JEREMY SCHIFELING

UNBREAKABLE

HOW TO AI-PROOF YOUR JOB SEARCH, CAREER, AND FUTURE

UNBREAKABLE

How to AI-Proof Your Job Search, Career, and Future

Dent & Type Books
437 Hope St.
Mountain View, CA 94041

Send feedback to jeremy@thejobinsiders.com

Ordering Information:
Quantity sales. Special discounts are available on quantity purchases by corporations, associations, and others. For details, contact the publisher at the address above.

Orders by U.S. trade bookstores and wholesalers.
Please contact Dent & Type Books:

Email: jeremy@thejobinsiders.com

Printed in the United States of America

Publisher's Cataloging-in-Publication data is available upon request

ISBN (Print): 979-8-9945181-0-6
ISBN (eBook): 979-8-9945181-1-3

First Edition

Editorial and visual development by Rose Ngo
Cover & Internal design by Caerus Kourt

FOR RUBY AND HANNAH

TABLE OF CONTENTS

HOW TO USE THIS BOOK..vii

PART 1: *What's Going On*..............................1
    CHAPTER 1: *What I've Seen*............................ 3
    CHAPTER 2: *What's Changed* 13

PART 2: *What to Do About It Now* 27
    CHAPTER 3: *Start with Strengths* 29
    CHAPTER 4: *Unite with Uniquely Human Skills*.......... 63
    CHAPTER 5: *Reinforce with Relevant AI*.................... 95
    CHAPTER 6: *Finish with Fellowship* 129

PART 3: *What to Do About It Next*...................161
    CHAPTER 7: *How to Get Your Next Job* 163
    CHAPTER 8: *How to Succeed in Your Next Job*....... 273
    CHAPTER 9: *How to Build Your Next Job*.................. 317
    CHAPTER 10: *The Most Important Lesson of All*...... 355

GET MY SURFBOT FOR FREE!..............................366
ACKNOWLEDGMENTS..367
ABOUT THE AUTHOR...369

HOW TO USE THIS BOOK

Here's the truth: Most people don't read career books cover-to-cover. They grab what they need right now and come back for the rest later.

That's totally fine. This book works both ways.

So before you dive in, find your path:

Need a job RIGHT NOW?
→ Focus on **Chapter 7**

Want to keep your current job?
→ Pay special attention to **Chapter 8**

Thinking about a side hustle?
→ Head on over to **Chapter 9**

Want the full transformation?
→ Read straight through and do the exercises

ONE QUICK SUGGESTION

No matter which path you choose, be sure to grab your free Surf Kit at THEJOBINSIDERS.COM/SURF. It's got every exercise, prompt, and tool to turbocharge your progress.

Instead of seeing AI as a threat, you'll see the wave coming - and understand exactly how to surf it.

Ready?

Grab your board. Let's go.

PART 1

WHAT'S GOING ON

1

WHAT I'VE SEEN

I'm like the Forrest Gump of the labor market.

Not because my career has been a box of chocolates - but because I've been there for all the pivotal labor moments of the 21st century:

- Earning a liberal arts degree right as the Computer Science revolution made traditional subjects seem obsolete...
- Working in New York's Financial District right as Occupy Wall Street protests arose during the Great Recession...
- Landing jobs in Silicon Valley right as those companies became the most valuable in the world...
- And working remotely four years before COVID made Work From Home normal for everyone!

But all those moments pale in comparison to the front-row seat I've had to the two biggest labor market disruptions of the 21st century.

And here's the wildest part: These two revolutions are mirror images of each other. The first gave unprecedented power to technical talent. The second is threatening to take it all away.

THE LINKEDIN REVOLUTION: WHEN TECH TALENT WON THE LOTTERY

When I took a job at LinkedIn right out of grad school in 2012, all my classmates thought I was crazy.

"You interned at Apple; you had offers at Amazon, Google, and Microsoft. What the heck is wrong with you?"

But as unsexy as LinkedIn seemed to my classmates, it was the hottest thing out there for a career nerd like me. That's because LinkedIn wasn't just another job board - it was fundamentally a *new* way for people to get jobs.

Here's what happened: If you had in-demand technical skills in the early 21st century, the emergence of LinkedIn meant that every recruiter in the world could now find you, reach out directly, and compete to win you over.

Think about that for a second. Before LinkedIn, if you were a programmer in Kansas City, your job options were basically limited to whatever companies happened to be in Kansas City. But suddenly, a recruiter at a hot startup in San Francisco could find your profile with a few clicks and slide into your DMs with a six-figure offer.

The results were intoxicating. I watched junior developers field multiple offers. I saw signing bonuses become the norm. I witnessed companies offering free sushi, nap pods, and laundry services just to attract talent.

Technical skills became the golden ticket. Everyone rushed to learn to code.

But here's the thing about golden tickets: *They're only valuable until underline everyone has one.*

THE AI REVOLUTION: WHEN THE TABLES TURNED

Fast forward exactly 10 years. I was working at Khan Academy, collaborating with young engineers who'd been recruited through LinkedIn for every job they'd ever had.

Then my boss, Sal Khan, got a call that changed everything.

The call was from this guy Sam, up in San Francisco. And he couldn't wait to show Sal "this cool new tool" that we could use to help more students learn.

The guy? Sam Altman.

That neat little tool? ChatGPT.

And the rest? History.

Because while we spent that year focused on incorporating ChatGPT into our learning platform, the real impact would be felt by all those engineers - and professionals everywhere - in ways we never expected.

Indeed, this second revolution is the diametric opposite of what the LinkedIn Revolution wrought. Instead of increasing *demand* for technical ability, AI increased the *supply*.

How? Think about what my engineering colleagues were doing in 2022:

- Writing technical specs
- Building landing pages
- Creating databases
- Analyzing user data

I couldn't do any of those things as a non-coder in 2022. Today? I can do every single one, aided by free AI platforms.

The marginal cost of adding technical bandwidth to a project has gone from those six-figure, sushi-laden offers to practically zero.

"Revolutionary" doesn't even begin to cover it.

THE DATA FINGERPRINTS OF DISRUPTION

But what matters more than the theory is how this is already playing out in real careers and real lives. The data tells a stark story:

The Decline in Programming Demand

Remember when "learn to code" was the answer to every career question? Not anymore (see Figure 1.1). According to *The Washington Post*, more than a quarter of computer-programming jobs (defined as basic coding roles) have vanished in just two years.

We now have fewer programmers in America than at any point since 1980.[1]

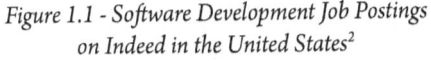

Figure 1.1 - Software Development Job Postings
on Indeed in the United States[2]

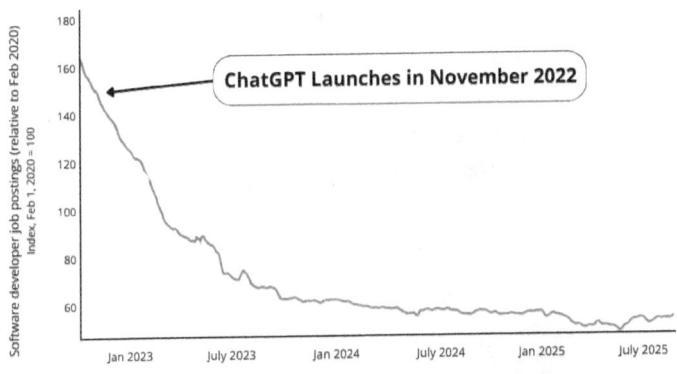

*The sharp decline in software developer job postings
immediately following ChatGPT's launch marks the moment
"learn to code" began turning into "learn to adapt."*

The New Grad Nightmare

It's not just programmers feeling the squeeze. New graduates are getting hit even harder.

1 "Computer-programming employment in U.S. falls to lowest since 1980," *The Washington Post*, March 14, 2025, https://www.washingtonpost.com/business/2025/03/14/programming-jobs-lost-artificial-intelligence/.

2 "Software Development Job Postings on Indeed in the United States," Federal Reserve Bank of St. Louis (FRED), December 2025.. https://fred.stlouisfed.org/series/IHLIDXUSTPSOFTDEVE

The Federal Reserve Bank of New York reports that, for the first time in recorded history, new college grads have a higher unemployment rate than the general public.[3]

While new grads used to have an advantage since they were so cheap to hire, in a world where AI can do many entry-level tasks for free, that traditional *advantage* has now become a distinct *disadvantage* (see Figure 1.2):

Figure 1.2 - The Recent Graduate Advantage
Has Flipped Into a Disadvantage[4]

The Recent Grad **Advantage...**

...Has Now Become a *Disadvantage*

〰️Total Unemployment minus Recent Grad Unemployment

The new-grad advantage flips: recent grads go from more employed than everyone else to more unemployed (yikes!).

3   "The Labor Market for Recent College Graduates," Federal Reserve Bank of New York, Q2 2025, https://www.newyorkfed.org/research/college-labor-market#--:overview.

4   U.S. Census Bureau and U.S. Bureau of Labor Statistics. Current Population Survey (IPUS).

The Woe-Is-Me Double Whammy

And you know who has it worst?

Not just programmers.

Not just new grads.

But new grad programmers.

Because the double whammy of an AI that can both code incredibly well - and do the most basic tasks super easily - is double trouble for the Learn to Code cohort.

So much so that they're now facing more than double the unemployment rate of my own troubled cohort - liberal arts grads (see Figure 1.3)![5]

Figure 1.3 - Unemployment Rate of Recent Graduates

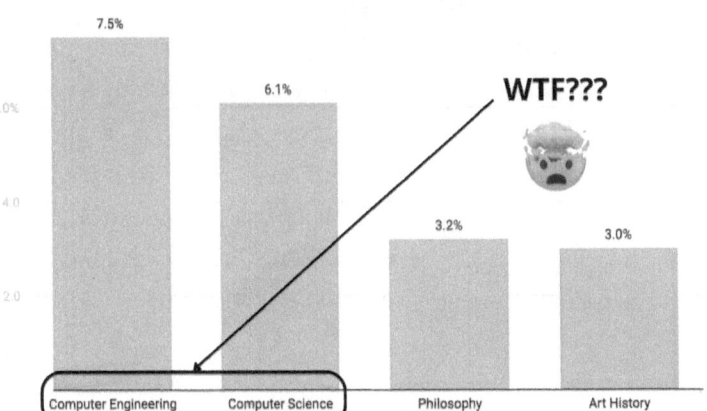

The plot twist nobody saw coming: CS and Engineering grads facing higher unemployment than Philosophy and Art History majors.

---

5   Ibid

YOUR GUIDE
THROUGH THE STORM

Now, I know this might sound terrifying. If you're reading this thinking, "Great, so my career is doomed?" - take a breath.

This isn't about everything you've learned becoming worthless. It's about understanding **the new rules of the game.**

I've been through two massive disruptions now. I've seen who thrives and who gets left behind. And here's what I've learned: The people who succeed aren't necessarily the smartest or the most skilled. They're the ones who see change coming and start adapting - even *before they need to.*

For example, think about all those statistics I just shared. They're not actually about AI *replacing* humans. They're about AI *changing* which human skills are scarce and valuable.

Programming jobs are declining because basic coding is no longer scarce. Entry-level positions are disappearing because routine tasks can be automated. But opportunities for people who can combine AI tools with deep human judgment are exploding.

Just look at Autodesk's analysis of the fastest-growing jobs.[6] Each one isn't just about AI - or a traditional skillset. But combining the two to become uniquely unstoppable (see Figure 1.4):

---

6   "2025 AI Jobs Report," Autodesk, June 2025, https://adsknews.autodesk. com/en/news/ai-jobs-report/.

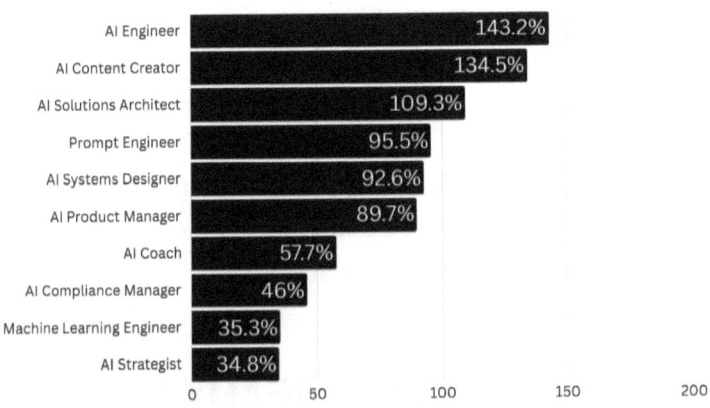

Figure 1.4 - Top 10 Fastest Growing AI job titles

*A leaderboard of the fastest-growing AI jobs - AKA the
roles riding the wave instead of getting wiped out by it.*

So the question isn't whether AI will change your career. It's
whether you'll be among the people who *harness* that change - or
get swept away by it.

WHAT'S COMING NEXT

This book is your roadmap to harnessing the power of this change.
Over the coming chapters, I'll show you:

- What's changed in how value gets created (hint: it's
  not just about being good at your job)
- What you need to do now to develop skills that *complement* rather than *compete* with AI

- What you need to do next to position yourself in the emerging economy
- The most important lesson of all for maintaining agency in an uncertain world

But most importantly, I'll help you develop something that no AI can replicate: unshakeable confidence in your ability to adapt and create value, no matter what comes next.

THE POWER IS ALREADY YOURS

Here's what I learned from having a front-row seat to both revolutions: Every massive disruption creates massive opportunity. The LinkedIn Revolution created millionaires out of people who happened to have the right technical skills at the right time. The AI Revolution will do the same for people who develop the right AI and humanistic skills right now.

So here we stand at that classic inflection point. The tools are here. The opportunities are emerging. The only question is: *Are you ready to grab them?*

Because while everyone else is panicking about AI taking their jobs, you're going to learn how to become the person AI makes more valuable, not less.

Ready to become unbreakable? **Let's dive in.**

2

WHAT'S CHANGED

Picture this: **It's** December 2024, and I'm sitting in a coffee shop in San Francisco, scrolling through my news feed when I nearly spit out my latte.

Marc Benioff, CEO of Salesforce - a $300 billion company, San Francisco's largest private employer, the crown jewel of enterprise software - just announced: "We're not adding any more software engineers next year."[7]

Wait, what?

That's like McDonald's saying they're done hiring people who can flip burgers. Or the NBA saying they don't need any more players who can dunk.

But here's the kicker - the part that everyone missed because they were too busy freaking out about the first statement. Benioff followed up with: "We really need to explain to people exactly the

---

7   "Salesforce bets on storytelling over engineering," Client/Server, January 13, 2025, https://www.clientserver.dev/p/salesforce-bets-on-storytelling-over.

value that we can achieve with AI. So, we will probably add another 1,000 to 2,000 salespeople."

I had to read that three times to make sure I wasn't hallucinating.

A company whose only product is software... is done hiring people to build software. But they're desperately hiring people to *sell* it.

That's when it hit me: The AI story isn't what any of us expected. Everyone thought AI would simply eliminate jobs - like some kind of employment asteroid hitting Earth. But the real story? It's way more interesting. And if you understand it, way more profitable for your career.

See, Salesforce didn't have too many workers. They had the wrong kind. And once you understand why, everything about the modern job market starts to make sense.

THE SCARCITY PRINCIPLE

OK, pop quiz time. (Yes, I'm that teacher who springs tests on you when you least expect them.)

 **POP QUIZ**

What is the primary driver of hiring + wages?

- A. Hard work
- B. Good intentions
- C. Scarce skills

If you picked C, congratulations - you don't just understand the world of hiring, you understand *the world*, period.

Here's the fundamental truth that took me years to figure out: Companies don't pay for what's common. They pay for what's *scarce*. It's Economics 101, but somehow we all forget it when we're updating our resumes.

For the last 25 years, software developers were the scarcest resource in business. Every company needed them. Few people could do the job. So developers commanded huge salaries, signing bonuses, and those infamous Silicon Valley perks (remember the Google ball pit in *The Internship* - guess what, it was real!).

Behold: The power of scarce skills!

But here's where the story gets wild: **AI just flipped the entire scarcity equation on its head.**

Because when something goes from scarce to abundant - from expensive to free - businesses stop paying premium prices for it. It's like what happened to encyclopedias. When information was scarce, people would pay thousands of dollars to get access - there was even an entire industry of salespeople dedicated to hawking encyclopedias door-to-door. Now, you get even more information for free instantly on Wikipedia. And the encyclopedia sales army? Gone the way of the dodo.

And that's exactly what Benioff was saying. It's not that coding doesn't matter. It's that basic coding is no longer scarce. AI can do it. So why pay six figures for something that costs nothing?

But here's the twist that changes everything: While AI made some things abundant, it made other things even more scarce. And *those* are the things companies are now desperate to find.

THE FOUR NEW SCARCITIES THAT CREATE VALUE

So if software development is no longer the bottleneck in our economic engine, what is?

After spending months analyzing job postings, talking to recruiters, and supporting thousands of students and professionals navigating this brave new world, I've identified four new types of scarcity that have emerged:

Scarcity #1: Expertise

Here's something that'll blow your mind: Stanford just released research showing that job openings for senior developers are growing at the exact same time that job openings for junior developers are crashing.[8]

Figure 2.1 - Employee Headcount Among
Software Developers, by Age

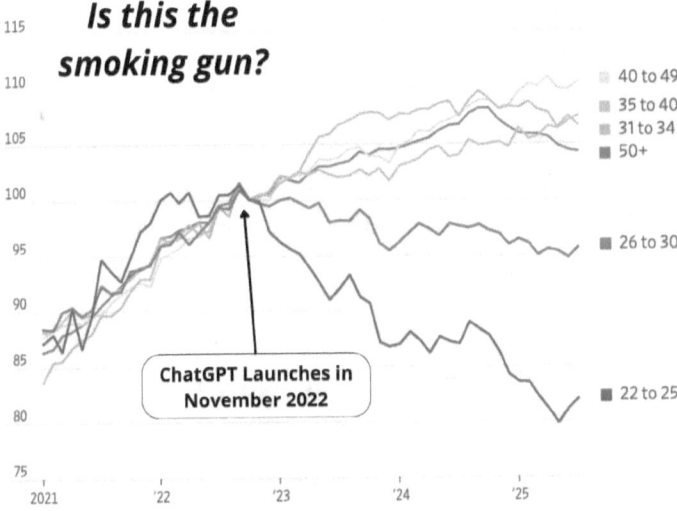

The junior-dev squeeze in one chart: younger developers take the hit after ChatGPT, while older cohorts continue up and to the right.

I know, I know - that seems totally backwards. If AI is replacing coders, shouldn't it replace the expensive senior ones first?

Nope. And here's why: AI is brilliant at doing basic things. It can write a for loop, create a landing page, draft a simple program. What

---

8   Brynjolfsson, Erik, Bharat Chandar, and Ruyu Chen. *Canaries in the Coal Mine? Six Facts about the Recent Employment Effects of Artificial Intelligence.* Stanford Digital Economy Lab Working Paper, August 26, 2025. https://digitaleconomy.stanford.edu/wp-content/uploads/2025/08/Canaries_BrynjolfssonChandarChen.pdf.

can't it do? Make architectural decisions. Understand complex trade-offs. Know when to break the rules. Figure out why the CEO's "simple request" is actually technically impossible - and diplomatically explain why!

Think of it this way: AI can follow a recipe perfectly. But it can't taste the soup and know it needs more salt. It can't look at wilting vegetables and adjust cooking time. It can't take three random ingredients and create something memorable.

In other words, the 50th percentile of skills is now fully automatable. But the 90th percentile is more valuable than ever.

The lesson? Don't be decent at something AI can do. Be exceptional at something it can't.

Scarcity #2: Human Skills

Even though AI can produce surprisingly effective technical output, it still lags far behind on some of the basic human skills we take for granted.

Take Google's much-vaunted AI Overviews. Even though they were trained on far more information than any human has ever had access to, they still made basic mistakes in understanding and empathy that would be incomprehensible to a 3-year old!

For instance, when asked how to make cheese stick to a pizza, its original solution was to mix in "about ⅛ cup of non-toxic glue (see Figure 2.2)."[9]

---

9   "Glue pizza and eat rocks: Google AI search errors go viral," BBC, May 24, 2024, https://www.bbc.com/news/articles/cd11gzejgz4o.

Figure 2.2 - What Happens When AI Knows
Facts but Lacks Human Judgment

Q cheese won't stick to pizza

Here are some tips to prevent cheese from sliding off pizza:

- Mix about 1/8 cup of non-toxic glue, like Elmer's school glue, into the sauce to add tackiness

> *A perfect reminder that putting a billion dollars into LLM training is no guarantee of actual wisdom!*

Effective? Yes.

Human? Absolutely not.

This makes human skills scarcer and more valuable than ever.

Look at the World Economic Forum's list of the most valuable skills for 2025:[10]

- *Empathy and active listening* (Can you understand your teammates' true needs, not just their prompts?)
- *Creative thinking* (Can you come up with ideas that aren't just regurgitations of existing data?)
- *Leadership and social influence* (Can you inspire actual humans, not just optimize workflows?)
- *Resilience and flexibility* (Can you adapt when everything goes sideways?)
- *Curiosity and lifelong learning* (Are you still asking "why" when AI just accepts "what"?)

---

10 "The Future of Jobs Report 2025," World Economic Forum, January 2025, https://www.weforum.org/reports/the-future-of-jobs-report-2025/.

Notice something? These aren't technical skills. They're human skills. Skills that require consciousness, emotion, lived experience. The kinds of skills you develop by living an actual life, not by training on internet data.

And so some of the first big AI pilots have crashed on those very shores of human experience. Whether it was Klarna rehiring human customer service agents after saying AI could do the work of 700 people ("AI gives us speed" but "talent gives us empathy," said the company's CEO)[11] or McDonald's doing away with AI-powered drive-thrus (after they ordered up such inhuman combos as "ice cream with ketchup and butter"),[12] the result is clear:

AI can process information. Only humans can create *meaning* from it.

Scarcity #3: AI Mastery

OK, here's where things get weird. While everyone and their grandmother is using AI, most people are using it completely *wrong*.

They're treating it like a magic wand: "Write me a cover letter!" "Make me a presentation!" "Do my homework!"

And what do they get? Generic garbage that screams "I used AI for this!" You know exactly what I'm talking about - those robotic LinkedIn posts that all sound the same, those cover letters that

---

11   "Klarna changes its AI tune and again recruits humans for customer service," CX Dive, May 9, 2025, https://www.customerexperiencedive.com/news/klarna-reinvests-human-talent-customer-service-AI-chatbot/747586.

12   "McDonald's is ending its test run of AI-powered drive-thrus with IBM," Associated Press, June 18, 2024, https://apnews.com/article/mcdonalds-ai-drive-thru-ibm-bebc898363f2d550e1a0cd3c682fa234.

could apply to any job at any company, those emails that make you feel like you're corresponding with The World's Most Boring Person ("In today's dynamic and rapidly evolving landscape, leveraging synergistic approaches is paramount for optimal outcomes...").

And ironically, research shows that people who use AI the most are often the ones who understand it the least.[13] They treat it like a crutch instead of a rocket booster.

But the people who actually know how to use AI as a force multiplier? They're becoming unstoppable.

Look at what Andrej Karpathy, former Tesla AI director, said about this: While everyone was using ChatGPT to write emails, he was using it to prototype entire software architectures, test edge cases, and validate complex mathematical proofs. Same tool, completely different results. He didn't replace his thinking with AI - he amplified it.[14]

Or consider the results from an AI experiment at Boston Consulting Group. The consultants who used AI as a crutch (i.e., using it to solve the problems they were supposed to solve themselves) performed 23% worse than the control group that used no AI. But those who used it on top of their existing expertise - to get even more creative and innovative? They outperformed the control group by 40%![15]

---

13 "The Less You Know About AI, the More You Are Likely to Use It," *The Wall Street Journal*, September 2, 2025, https://www.wsj.com/tech/ai/ai-adoption-study-7219d0a1.

14 "How I Use LLMs," YouTube, February 27, 2025, https://www.youtube.com/watch?v=EWvNQjAaOHw

15 "How People Can Create—and Destroy—Value with Generative AI," Boston Consulting Group, September 21, 2023, https://www.bcg.com/publications/2023/how-people-create-and-destroy-value-with-gen-ai.

The difference? Understanding that AI isn't a replacement for thinking - it's an amplifier for it. And companies will pay top dollar for people who get this distinction.

Scarcity #4: Trust & Relationships

In a world of deepfakes, AI-generated content, and digital everything, you know what's become incredibly scarce? Trust.

More than two-thirds of business leaders now say that trust has become much more important than ever before when making decisions.[16] Not data. Not analysis. Trust.

Think about that. We have more data than ever. More analysis tools than ever. More information than ever. And what do executives care about most? Whether they can trust the person across the table.

Why? Because when anyone can generate a perfect resume, the job goes to whoever has the strongest relationship. When AI can write flawless proposals, the contract goes to whomever the client trusts most. When every email could be written by a bot, the deals go to people who show up as actual humans.

Don't believe me? Just look at global business travel.

If you've ever earned Platinum Status on an airline, you know that it's one of those "rewards" you actually *don't* want to earn. After

---

16 "IPA and Financial Times Study Reveals Trust Is Second Most Powerful Business Driver," Little Black Book, July 10, 2025, https://lbbonline.com/news/Study-from-IPA-and-Financial-Times-Reveals-Trust-Is-Second-Most-Powerful-Business-Driver

all, no one locks themselves in a little metal tube shooting through the stratosphere for 100,000+ miles for the fun of it!

And yet, business travel is now expected to be 12% higher this year than in the year before COVID.[17]

Why?

Because research has consistently shown that outside sales representatives (i.e., those meeting in-person with clients) have a closing rate 2X that of their inside (i.e., HQ-based) counterparts.

Which means relationships aren't just nice to have. They're the ultimate competitive advantage.

THE WAVE IS COMING

Picture this: You're standing on a beach, and someone points to the horizon. "See that?" they say. "That's a HUGE wave."

What do you do?

Most people fall into three camps:

1. **The Deniers** - "Nah - it's just a mirage. I'm going to keep building my sand castle and everything will be fine..."

2. **The Runners** - "Yikes - that freaks me out. I'm going home to huddle under my blankets!"

3. **The Surfers** - "Holy cow, that's crazy... but it could also be amazing." So they grab their boards and paddle out.

---

17 "Business travel spend to hit $1.57t in 2025," Business Travel News Europe, July 22, 2025, https://www.businesstravelnewseurope.com/Management/GBTA-downgrades-business-travel-growth-expectations.

The Deniers' sand castles get completely wiped out. The Runners survive but miss out on the opportunity. And the Surfers? They're about to ride that wave to heights that wouldn't have been possible before.

Which one are you going to be?

YOUR ROADMAP TO RIDING THE WAVE

Look, I get it. When you're staring at that AI wave, your first instinct might be to run. Or to pretend it's not there. Those are natural, human responses to massive change.

But here's what I've learned from my own journey through two career revolutions: The people who thrive aren't the ones who avoid change. They're the ones who learn to dance with it.

So how do you get the confidence to tango with the change? To surf the AI wave?

It all comes back to scarcity.

If that's what companies and the world value, that's what you focus on.

So without further ado, here's SURF - your step-by-step guide to developing the four types of scarce skills that matter most:

S **Start with Strengths** - Stop trying to be decent at what AI can do. Instead, develop deep expertise that puts you in the top 10% of your field. (I'll show you exactly how to identify and develop these strengths in Chapter 3.)

U **Unite with Uniquely Human Skills** - Master the soft skills that AI can't replicate. The ones that require actual consciousness, emotion, and lived experience. (Chapter 4 is your playbook for this.)

R **Reinforce with Relevant AI** - Learn to use AI as a multiplier, not a crutch. Most people are doing this completely wrong - I'll show you how to do it right. (Chapter 5 breaks this down.)

F **Finish with Fellowship** - Build the relationships and trust that matter more than ever. In a world of digital everything, human connections are gold. (Chapter 6 is your ultimate networking guide.)

So hop on your board.
The wave is almost here.
Let's get ready to ride.

PART 2

WHAT TO DO ABOUT IT NOW

3

START WITH STRENGTHS

Alright, **reality check** time.

If you're like most people, you just read about the changing scarcity landscape and thought one of two things:

1. "I'm doomed! All my coding skills are worthless!" (Spoiler: Wrong)
2. "Great! I'm not a coder, so AI can't replace me!" (Also wrong)

Both reactions miss the point entirely.

AI isn't going to laser target one profession for demolition while leaving all others unscathed. It's going to come for the mediocre professional *across* professions.

So the first AI-proofing step isn't about acquiring new skills. It's about understanding what you're already great at.

And before you roll your eyes thinking this is some feel-good, find-your-passion nonsense, let me stop you right there. This is about cold, hard strategy. Because in the AI age, being "pretty good" at something is a death sentence for your career.

THE 50TH PERCENTILE PROBLEM

Let me hit you with some uncomfortable math that'll make you rethink everything about your career strategy.

AI is currently at about the 50th percentile for most tasks. Think about what that means. It can write a decent email – not great, not terrible, just... decent. It can code a basic app that works but won't win any awards. It can create a passable design that won't embarrass anyone but won't impress anyone either. It can analyze standard data and produce standard insights.

Now here's the career-killer question: Where are you on that percentile scale?

If you're at the 50th percentile – if you're average – you're competing directly with something that costs nothing and works 24/7. No sick days. No coffee breaks. No complaining about the workload.

That's not a competition. That's a massacre.

But here's where it gets interesting (and where your opportunity lies): AI really struggles to get from decent to excellent. It just can't hit the 90th percentile that we demand from truly great professionals.

Sure, it can write a memo. But how many AI-generated books have you read late into the night like Stephen King's *The Stand*?

Sure, it can spit out a picture. But how many AI-generated images have crowds lining up at the art museum like Van Gogh's *Starry Night*?

Sure, it can code an app. But how many AI-generated video games have you spent hundreds of hours mastering like *Super Mario Bros.*?

Because AI is decent at almost everything, you need to be **exceptional** at something. And not just marginally better – you want to aim for the top 10% to give yourself a comfortable margin.

That means finding skills that are hard for everyone else but easy for you. The things you're naturally drawn to. The stuff that doesn't *feel like work*.

YOUR SUPERPOWER IS HIDING IN PLAIN SIGHT

Most people think their strength is their job title. "I'm an accountant." "I'm a marketer." "I'm a teacher."

Wrong. Those are just containers for your actual superpower.

Take Howard Schultz.

In 1987, Schultz bought Starbucks when it had just 17 stores. Naturally, he thought he was in the coffee business. **He was wrong.**

Because every competitor focused on selling the best coffee beans, the best cup. But sitting in a Milan espresso bar, Schultz realized his superpower wasn't selling coffee – it was creating a "third place" between work and home where people felt they belonged.

So what did he do about it?

He didn't hire better coffee experts. He trained the same baristas to remember names, write personal messages on cups, and create community. Starbucks grew to 38,000 stores not because they had the best coffee, but because Schultz understood he wasn't in the coffee business - he was in the human connection business.

I discovered this myself when I was teaching. I thought my strength was lesson planning – I had these elaborate, color-coded binders that would make Marie Kondo weep with joy. But when I paid attention to what actually energized me, it wasn't the planning. It was those moments when a struggling student suddenly understood a concept. When their face lit up with that "aha!" moment.

My superpower wasn't organizing information. It was translating complex ideas into simple understanding. That realization led me from teaching kindergarteners their ABCs to teaching millions of people about careers through LinkedIn and my own business.

Today, when people ask me what I do, I don't say "I'm a marketer" or "I'm an educator." I say "I help people build great careers and lives."

FINDING YOUR NORTH STAR: THE IKIGAI FRAMEWORK

Before we dive into tactics, you need to understand where you're heading. The Japanese have a concept called ikigai (生き甲斐) - your "reason for being" or purpose in life (see Figure 3.1).

Picture four overlapping circles:

- What you're **great at** (your strengths)
- What you **love** (your passions)

- What you can be **paid for** (your job title)
- What the world **needs** (your future)

Your ikigai lives at the center where all four circles intersect. It's your career sweet spot - the place where you can be both fulfilled and financially successful.

Figure 3.1 - The Ikigai Venn Diagram

The Ikigai Venn diagram: what you love + what you're good at + what pays + what the world needs = the career sweet spot.

Research from Japanese longitudinal studies shows that people who've found their ikigai have a 36% lower risk of developing dementia and 31% lower risk of functional disability.[18] Studies also show ikigai is associated with reduced cardiovascular disease mortality and longer life expectancy.[19]

The problem? Most people only focus on one or two circles. They chase money without considering their strengths. Or they follow their passion without checking if anyone will pay for it.

We're going to systematically work through each circle to find your unique intersection.

INTRODUCING YOUR SURF KIT

As we tackle each circle, I don't want you just to *think* about these concepts. I want you to take action - today!

But let's face it: That's the exact thing that's **super hard** for us.

Because thousands of generations of evolution have bred our species to be:

- Terrible at **long-term thinking** (all our ancestors who developed elaborate plans for dealing with the Ice Age got wiped out while those who focused on gathering food *today* survived)

---

18 Okuzono, S. S., Shiba, K., Kim, E. S., Shirai, K., Kondo, N., Fujiwara, T., Kondo, K., Lomas, T., Trudel-Fitzgerald, C., Kawachi, I., & VanderWeele, T. J. (2022). "Ikigai and subsequent health and wellbeing among Japanese older adults: Longitudinal outcome-wide analysis." Lancet Regional Health - Western Pacific, 21, 100391. https://doi.org/10.1016/j.lanwpc.2022.100391

19 Sone, T., Nakaya, N., Ohmori, K., Shimazu, T., Higashiguchi, M., Kakizaki, M., ... & Tsuji, I. (2008). "Sense of life worth living (ikigai) and mortality in Japan: Ohsaki Study." Psychosomatic Medicine, 70(6), 709-715. https://pubmed.ncbi.nlm.nih.gov/18596247/.

- Allergic to anything that requires **hard mental work** (our brain uses up 2% of our body weight but 20% of its energy, which means we've evolved to crave the things that don't ask much of it - TikTok anyone? - but dread the things that force it into action - how'd you like to do your taxes instead?)[20]

So to overcome these innate challenges, we're actually going to turn AI into our *frenemy*. Yes, it poses massive existential threats to our future. And yet, it's also the best single way to overcome the above. After all, AI doesn't have our evolutionary baggage so long-term thinking and hard mental work are all just another day at the office/data center.

Thus, for every single exercise below, you'll find a corresponding prompt that you can copy-and-paste directly from your Surf Kit - which is available for free at THEJOBINSIDERS.COM/SURF.

So grab that right now and then get ready to overcome our evolutionary kryptonite: Thinking hard today to live large tomorrow!

STAGE 1: DISCOVERING WHAT YOU'RE GREAT AT

Pop quiz time again!

---

20 "Your Brain Didn't Evolve to Think. Here's What It Does Best," Next Big Idea Club, November 25, 2020, https://nextbigideaclub.com/magazine/brain-didnt-evolve-think-heres-best

 **POP QUIZ**

What percentage of people think they're above-average drivers?

A. 50%
B. 75%
C. 93%

If you guessed C, you're absolutely right. That's because even though your answer is mathematically impossible, the Dunning-Kruger effect reveals that we're poor judges of our own skills - and that the least competent people are often the most confident about their abilities![21]

Which means that even if you think you're terrible at something, you might actually be great (since Dunning and Kruger also found that high performers tend to *underestimate* their abilities). Or vice-versa!

So when it comes time to discover your strengths, forget trusting your gut. Instead, recognize that outside observers are 2.5 times more likely to predict our performance than we are.[22] So reach for your handy-dandy Surf Kit and then get ready to dive into your world - as seen by others.

---

21 Justin Kruger and David Dunning, "Unskilled and Unaware of It: How Difficulties in Recognizing One's Own Incompetence Lead to Inflated Self-Assessments," *Journal of Personality and Social Psychology* 77, no. 6 (1999): 1121-1134, https://doi.org/10.1037/0022-3514.77.6.1121.

22 Mount, Michael K., and Steven E. Scullen. "Multisource Feedback Ratings: What Do They Really Measure?" In Personnel Psychology in Practice, edited by Kevin R. Murphy and Jeanette N. Cleveland, 155-176. San Francisco: Jossey-Bass, 2001.

Step 1: Start by gathering any testimonials/reviews you've received. These include LinkedIn Recommendations (instructions for downloading these are included in the Surf Kit), on-the-job performance reviews, and letters of recommendation.

Step 2: Upload the files to your preferred AI platform. Note that you can use any platform these days since they're all trained on similar data with similar techniques. And you definitely don't need a premium account - our goal is to help *you* get richer, not the AI companies!

Step 3: Because we're working with personal data, the Surf Kit includes full instructions for preventing your AI platform from incorporating your data into its model. Take that, Skynet!

Step 4: Copy this prompt from the Surf Kit and paste it into your AI:

PROMPT

```
What are [your name]'s strengths?

Put extra emphasis on others' feedback,
including the following attached files:

-Their LinkedIn recommendations
-Their performance reviews
-Their letters of recommendation
```

> Please summarize into a Top 5 list and
> provide sourcing/specific evidence that
> supports each strength.

Step 5: Boom. You now have a great starting place for your strengths - according to people who've actually worked with you, not just the massively untrustworthy voice in our heads.

 AI OUTPUT

Top 5 Strengths of Jeremy Schifeling

1. Deep Expertise & Knowledge Sharing

Jeremy is consistently praised for his mastery of LinkedIn, career strategy, and emerging tools like AI. More importantly, he shares that knowledge generously, making complex topics accessible.

- *"He has a deep understanding of his field and provided clear, useful advice that made a real difference."* **— Claudio Klaus**

- *"Jeremy is a WEALTH of knowledge in the career development space. His materials… are ALWAYS packed with value giving me new perspectives."* **— Adam Shpall, MBA, CUCC**

- *"Jeremy shared his vast knowledge of and from LinkedIn along with AI tools to aid with folks' search, networking, and professional branding."* — **Scott Turner, EMBA**

2. Inspiring Mentor & Coach

His mentees highlight both his career guidance and his ability to instill confidence and persistence. Jeremy is not just a coach but a mentor who meets people where they are.

- *"Jeremy was the mentor I needed to get out of my comfort zone… He will not let you sell yourself short and will constantly challenge you to be the best version of yourself."* — **James Park**

- *"Without him, I wouldn't have been able to power through the roller coaster of emotions in the career switch with such persistence. He boosted my confidence… to land a job on my second in-person interview ever."* — **Adam Niekras, MBA**

An AI-generated "strengths report" that turns scattered testimonials into a clear list of your real superpowers (with receipts).

STAGE 2: IDENTIFYING WHAT YOU LOVE

Here's where most career advice goes wrong. It tells you to "follow your passions"... without ever helping you identify what your passions actually are!

So rather than guess at your passions ("Umm... I guess I like... uh... video games and stuff"), you need to become a Flow Detective.

"Flow" is the state of deep engrossment that comes when you're working on something that truly matters to you. Coined by the psychologist Mihaly Csikszentmihalyi, here are some of the hallmarks:

- The challenge is in the Goldilocks Zone - neither too boring, nor too hard
- You experience intense focus - i.e., being "in the zone"
- Time flies by and you don't even notice

And here's the best part: Because Csikszentmihalyi's research shows that you're more likely to enter flow states when you're tackling something you're passionate about, its presence is a key indicator of what truly matters to you.[23]

So, to fill out this circle in your Ikigai diagram, let's go back to your Surf Kit and complete the following exercise:

---

23 Csikszentmihalyi, Mihaly. Flow: The Psychology of Optimal Experience. New York: Harper & Row, 1990.

Start with Strengths

Step 1: Open your calendar and to-do list from last week

Step 2: Rate each event/task with an emoji:

- 👍 = "Time flew by, I could do this all day"
- 🙂 = "Meh, it was fine"
- 👎 = "I wanted to fake my own death to escape"

Step 3: Copy this into your preferred AI platform:

😛 PROMPT

```
Here are my recent activities rated by flow
states or the lack thereof:

👍    Energy-giving: [list them]
🙂    Neutral: [list them]
👎    Energy-draining: [list them]

Based on this analysis, please generate a
Top 3 list of passions that drive energy
and flow.
```

Step 4: Voila! By following your energy trail, you've actually come right back to your North Star: The things that light you up. And note: These may or may not be similar to the key Strengths you identified in the previous exercise. After all, the whole point of Ikigai is to find the union of your strengths and passions - not just overindex on one or the other.

🤔 PROMPT

Here are my recent activities rated by flow states or the lack thereof:

👍 *Energy-giving:*
Leading career workshops, recording a podcast about how Gen Z and jobs, coming up with travel plans for the family

🙂 *Neutral:*
Meeting with prospective clients, coming up with LinkedIn posts, responding to forum messages

👎 *Energy-draining:*
Working on invoices, getting through email, PTA fundraising work

Based on this analysis, please generate a Top 3 list of passions that drive energy and flow.

An image-coded energy journal that makes your "love it / meh / hate it" patterns impossible to ignore.

🤖 AI OUTPUT

Here's a synthesis of your flow-state analysis, distilled into your **Top 3 passions that drive energy and flow:**

1. Teaching and Sharing Knowledge

- **Why it stands out:** Leading career workshops and recording a podcast both gave you energy. These activities center on helping others grow, sparking new ideas, and amplifying your voice.

- **Flow trigger:** You thrive when you're facilitating, storytelling, and engaging with audiences – especially when it involves career development, generational shifts (like Gen Z), and big-picture thinking.

2. **Creative Planning and Visioning**

- **Why it stands out:** Designing travel plans for your family energized you. That's not just logistics – it's visioning, weaving experiences together, and imagining possibilities.

- **Flow trigger:** When you can take raw ideas (whether trips, projects, or strategies) and shape them into exciting, actionable plans.

AI pulling themes from your journal to spotlight the passions that consistently put you in flow.

STAGE 3: FINDING WHAT YOU CAN BE PAID FOR

Now we get to the magic step: combining your strengths and passions to find roles that can actually get you paid.

Not only is this step essential to your future financial success, it also aligns exactly with what matters to your key audience: Recruiters.

As we'll discuss in Part 3, when it comes time to find your next job, Recruiters are the gatekeepers you need to understand and serve above all others.

And how do you think Recruiters look for top candidates?

Is it possible that they search for people with "leadership strengths" and "a passion for finance?"

Heck no!

They go right into their Applicant Tracking System or LinkedIn Recruiter account and search for a "Chief Financial Officer:"

Figure 3.2 - How Recruiters Actually Search: job title First

Show Advanced Search Options

Job title *	Chief Financial Officer	
Entering a job title is highly recommended	(e.g., Sales, Accountant, Engineer)	
Years of experience	10+	Nice to have
	(e.g., 4, 2-3, 5+, <8)	
Location	10001, New York, NY	within 50 miles
	(i.e., city, state, OR ZIP Code)	
Skills/Keywords	Financial Accounting	Required
Enter terms related to candidates industry or	Remote Team Management	Required
expertise (e.g. java, telesales, call center, retail,	Econometric Modeling	Nice to have
SOX)	Add another skill or keyword	

Recruiters always keep their eyes on the job title prize - and so should you!

Luckily, you've got the world's most knowledgeable career coach on your side: AI. Because what it lacks in empathy, it makes up for in encyclopedic knowledge of job titles from Apiarists (AKA

Beekeepers) to Zymurgists (AKA Brewers). Just follow these steps to see which ones are right for you:

Step 1: Plug your Strengths and Passions into this prompt:

PROMPT

My strengths: [list from Stage 1]

My passions: [list from Stage 2]

Generate 10 specific job titles that leverage my strengths AND engage my passions.

For each title, include an overview of the role, the typical salary range in MY LOCATION, and why this role aligns with my strengths and passions.

AI OUTPUT

Here's a tailored **Top 10 job titles** list that combines your strengths and passions, with role overviews, Bay Area salary ranges, and alignment notes:

1. Learning & Development Director

- **Overview:** Leads company-wide training, talent development, and leadership programs. Designs and delivers learning strategies that support growth and engagement.

- **Salary (SF Bay Area):** $160k-$220k
- **Alignment:** Perfect for your expertise in knowledge sharing, coaching, and impactful communication. You'd be energizing teams through teaching and mentorship.

2. Chief Learning Officer (CLO)

- **Overview:** Executive-level role shaping organizational learning strategy, driving culture change, and building talent pipelines.
- **Salary:** $220k-$300k+
- **Alignment:** Leverages your strategic visioning and student-centered leadership. A platform for thought leadership and creating large-scale impact.

A "top job titles for you" list generated from your strengths and interests - i.e., career matchmaking, minus the awkward first date.

Step 2: To prioritize, you can sort it by the key attributes of a great life that matter to you (e.g., compensation, work-life balance, travel, social impact, etc.):

PROMPT

Generate a ranked table of these roles sorted in descending order based on my key goals: [insert attributes]

AI OUTPUT

Here's your **stack-ranked table**, ordered by
best fit for **Work-Life Balance** and **Social
Impact** (descending):

RANK	ROLE	WORK-LIFE BALANCE	SOCIAL IMPACT	WHY IT FITS
🏅 1	Executive Coach (Gen Z & Future of Work)	High	High	You set your schedule and directly transform leaders and organizations.
🏅 2	Corporate Workshop Facilitator	High	High	Flexible, project-based, and energizing group impact through learning.
🏅 3	Professional Speaker / Thought Leader	High-Moderate	High	Autonomy with high visibility; influences broad audiences.

*A comparison table that ranks roles by work-life balance and impact -
because "good fit" should include more than just compensation.*

Step 3: Finally, to cut your original list down to a more
manageable size, you can ask for the following deep dive:

PROMPT

For the Top 5 jobs in my table, please provide a deep dive into each, including a typical day, the kinds of people who succeed in this work, and the kinds of people who struggle with it.

AI OUTPUT

Perfect — let's do a **deep dive into your Top 5 roles** based on **Work-Life Balance + Social Impact**.

1. Executive Coach (Gen Z & Future of Work)

Typical Day

- **Morning:**
- Prep for 1:1 client sessions, review notes from prior conversations, tailor coaching frameworks.
- **Midday:** Conduct 2-4 coaching sessions (executives, managers, or emerging leaders).
- **Afternoon:** Networking calls, business development, writing content (articles, LinkedIn, podcast).
- **Evening:** Often free unless clients are international.

Who Succeeds

- Empathetic listeners who can ask powerful, open-ended questions.

- Self-starters who enjoy building their own practice and reputation.

- People energized by deep 1:1 conversations and long-term transformation.

Who Struggles

- Those who dislike sales, client acquisition, or unstructured income streams.

- People who prefer fixed roles and stability over entrepreneurial freedom.

A day-in-the-life breakdown of an executive coach

Step 4: With all of this occupational data at your fingertips, try to narrow your list of potential roles down to a Top 3. While it's totally fine to have more or fewer options at this point, there are still two filters left - so we want to leave enough flexibility to make a few final cuts.

And by the way, this isn't just a fun, little AI exercise. Instead, it links back to cold, hard cash. That's because research shows that working in a role that fits your strengths and passions is directly correlated with higher compensation. Specifically, it's equivalent to getting an extra month's worth of pay every year.[24] Not too shabby for a few minutes of prompting!

---

24 Kristof-Brown, Amy L., Ryan D. Zimmerman, and Erin C. Johnson. 2005. "Consequences of Individuals' Fit at Work: A Meta-Analysis of Person–Job, Person–Organization, Person–Group, and Person–Supervisor Fit." Personnel Psychology 58 (2): 281–342. https://onlinelibrary.wiley.com/doi/10.1111/j.1744-6570.2005.00672.x

STAGE 4: UNDERSTANDING WHAT THE WORLD NEEDS

Now comes the ultimate test: Not just understanding what the world will pay you for today, but also what it needs *tomorrow*.

In other words: **The AI Test.**

That's because, as the first two chapters laid out, the world is changing fast. And so it makes no sense to commit to a role today that will likely be obsolete in a few years.

To make sure that you're prepared, start by understanding which jobs are most resistant to automation. Specifically, which jobs are most HUMAN.

To that end, I've created a rubric to help break down what makes a role most AI-proof, based on the human skill scarcity principles from the preceding chapter:

H   **High-stakes decisions**
(Will someone die/lose millions if you mess up?)

U   **Unpredictable situations**
(Is there fresh chaos to manage every day?)

M   **Managing relationships**
(Are there actual humans involved?)

A   **Aesthetics and creativity**
(Does performance hinge on taste or ideas?)

N   **Needs presence**
(Is in-person work required?)

Here's how to apply it:

Step 1: Run the following prompt to score your potential roles:

 **PROMPT**

> Generate a table that ranks [my desired roles] based on the following criteria:
>
> - High-stakes decisions
> - Unpredictable situations
> - Managing relationships
> - Aesthetics and creativity
> - Needs presence
>
> Score each role on a scale of 1-10 (1 is not present at all in the job, 10 is massively present) and sort in descending order by a combined HUMAN score across all criteria.

AI OUTPUT

AI-Proofing Role Rankings

RANK	ROLE	HIGH-STAKES DECISIONS	UNPREDICTABLE SITUATIONS	MANAGING RELATIONSHIPS	AESTHETICS & CREATIVITY	NEEDS PRESENCE	TOTAL (50)
1	Community Builder / Member Engagement	5	8	10	7	7	37
2	Corporate Workshop Facilitator	5	7	9	7	7	35
3	Head of Career Services (Univ/EdTech)	6	7	9	6	6	34

Build your own AI "crystal ball" by examining what will make a role AI-proof tomorrow, today!

Step 2: To interpret the scores, consider this guide:

- *Above 35?* You're golden. Playing to human strengths FTW!
- *25-35?* You're in the gray zone. It can still be good - you just need to be great.
- *Below 25?* Warning! Proceed cautiously but be sure to have a Plan B.

Note that these scores are just guides - not hard-and-fast rules for the job you must pursue. In other words, don't write-off a job you're genuinely excited about just because it scores low.

Why?

Well, consider the plight of programmers and plumbers...

Shouldn't I Just Become a Plumber?

No sooner did Generative AI show off its white collar chops than the headlines started screaming:

- *NBC News:* "Blue-collar jobs are gaining popularity as AI threatens office work"[25]
- *The Wall Street Journal:* "How Gen Z Is Becoming the Toolbelt Generation"[26]

---

25 "Blue-Collar Jobs Are Gaining Popularity as AI Threatens Office Work," NBC News, August 16 2025. https://www.nbcnews.com/business/business-news/ai-which-jobs-are-skilled-trades-protected-what-to-know-rcna223249

26 "How Gen Z Is Becoming the Toolbelt Generation," *The Wall Street Journal*, April 1, 2024. https://www.wsj.com/lifestyle/careers/gen-z-trades-jobs-plumbing-welding-a76b5e43

And, of course...

- *Hindustan Times*: " 'Be a plumber': Godfather of AI reveals the jobs that AI won't replace anytime soon"[27]

But what you might have missed in that deluge was this little headline from *Fortune*: "Gen Z is ditching college for 'more secure' trade jobs—but building inspectors, electricians and plumbers actually have the worst unemployment."[28]

That's right - the very jobs that everyone is fleeing to are already the most challenging to win.

Which takes us right back to where we started: **Scarcity.**

The minute that everyone floods into a role, those skills are no longer scarce.

Don't believe me?

Just ask all the unemployed CS majors who flooded - and overflooded - that field.

So before you rush out to master plumbing, remember that your strengths and passions are actually more predictive of your success than the role you choose. Indeed, research shows that < 25% of wage variation comes from the kinds of jobs people pick - whereas 50%+ comes from the performance they uniquely bring to that job.[29]

---

27 " 'Be a plumber': Godfather of AI reveals the jobs that AI won't replace anytime soon," *Hindustan Times*, June 17, 2025. https://www.hindustantimes.com/trending/be-a-plumber-godfather-of-ai-reveals-the-jobs-that-ai-won-t-replace-anytime-soon-101750149477574.html

28 "Gen Z is ditching college for 'more secure' trade jobs—but building inspectors, electricians and plumbers actually have the worst unemployment," *Fortune*, July 2, 2025, https://fortune.com/2025/07/02/gen-z-ditching-college-secure-trade-jobs-blue-collar-electricians-and-plumbers-worst-unemployment-rate-than-office-jobs/.

29 Song, Jae, David J. Price, Fatih Guvenen, Nicholas Bloom, and Till von Wachter. "Firming Up Inequality." *Quarterly Journal of Economics* 134, no. 1 (2019): 1–50. https://academic.oup.com/qje/article/134/1/5197018.

So unless you're genuinely awesome at pipefitting and passionate about fixtures, remember that the AI Test is one part of your larger Ikigai equation - not the only driver!

STAGE 5: TESTING YOUR IKIGAI HYPOTHESIS

So how do you know which job to actually pursue?

Recognize that, at this point, your Venn Diagram ikigai overlap is just a *hypothesis*. And like any good hypothesis, it needs to get tested with real data.

And in this age of AI hallucinations, what's the realest of the real?

Real people.

As in, go out and talk to them!

Because while AI can give you great ideas, it can't give you the visceral, gut-feel that comes from talking to someone who's doing that job right now. And most importantly, it can't give you the Vulcan Mind-Meld where you start to imagine yourself doing the job mid-conversation.

Because that's where the rubber hits the road. And this is your roadmap:

Step 1: Pick your Top 2 roles from Stage 4

Step 2: For each role, find people you know on LinkedIn doing that job today by searching for the job title and filtering for 1st Degree Connections:

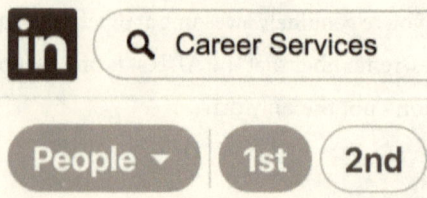

Searching for the job title and 1st Degree Connections is the perfect combo to find insiders who'd be happy to help you learn!

Step 3: Reach out to at least three people you want to learn from with a message like this:

> Hi [name],
>
> I'm exploring [job title] careers and would love to learn about your path!
>
> Any chance you have even 10 minutes for a quick chat next week?
>
> Even a little time would make a huge difference as I'm so curious about your journey.
>
> Thanks for considering!
>
> [your name]

Step 4: If you don't have any 1st Degree Connections, just switch to 2nd Degree (i.e., friends of friends) and reach out to your mutual connection like so:

Start with Strengths

A 2nd Degree search on LinkedIn immediately turns up friends of friends - so you don't have to ever do awkward cold outreach.

Hi [name],

Would you mind introducing me to NAME?

I'm currently exploring [job title] careers and would love to learn from their experience.

To make it easier, I've included a little message below that you can forward them and just Cc me on.

Thanks for considering!

[your name]

Below is an intro message you can send to the contact:

Hi [name],

My name is [your name] and I'm a friend of X's. I was excited to ask for an introduction because I'm exploring [job title] careers and would love to learn from people actually doing the role.

That said, I know you must be very busy but is there any chance you have even 10 minutes for a quick chat next week?

Even a little time would make a huge difference as I'm so curious about your journey.

Thanks for considering!

[your name]

Step 5: Once you've set-up three interviews for each role, be sure to come into each conversation with an Ikigai Mindset. In other words, don't just find out whether your connection loves their job - find out whether *you'll* love their job too!

To that end, be sure to download your connection's LinkedIn profile (Click More → Save to PDF) and then upload it to AI with the following prompt:

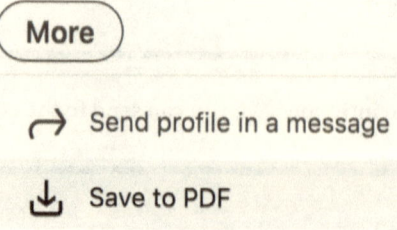

LinkedIn prevents most AIs from searching profiles directly - but by downloading profiles to PDF first, you can still leverage this powerful information.

Generate 10 questions for this professional to help me decide whether their role fits my:

Strengths:

Passions:

Goals:

Example:

Generate 10 questions for this professional to help me decide whether their role fits my:

- *Strengths:* Deep Expertise & Knowledge Sharing, Inspiring Mentor & Coach
- *Passions:* Teaching and Sharing Knowledge, Creative Planning and Visioning
- *Goals:* Work-Life Balance, Social Impact

[attached PDF of profile]

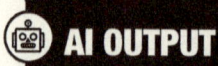
AI OUTPUT

Here are **10 tailored questions** you can ask this professional to see if their role and approach align with your strengths, passions, and goals:

About Knowledge Sharing & Mentorship

1. In your coaching practice, how do you create opportunities for deep knowledge exchange rather than surface-level advice?

2. What approaches do you use to inspire and guide others in ways that go beyond traditional career coaching?

...

This is the ultimate triangulation - identify the key connections between your desired role, your strengths + passions, and your insider contact.

Step 6: As you conduct these conversations, pay just as much attention to your gut as your connection. That's because research shows that the best decision-making often comes from a blend of good data AND intuition.[30] And since we've already generated reams of data via AI, it's time to complement that with the real-time indicators we're getting via these conversations.

---

30 Daniel Kahneman and Gary Klein, "Conditions for Intuitive Expertise: A Failure to Disagree," *American Psychologist* 64, no. 6 (2009): 515-526.

So if you find yourself leaning in as you hear about these roles, don't ignore that intuition. Instead, use it to come right back to where we started: Your ikigai.

Because what does ikigai mean?

Basically, a reason to jump out of bed in the morning!

Which means you owe it to your future self not just to find a role that withstands the AI deluge, but that serves as your internal alarm clock - that jolt of intrinsic motivation that sets you off on a path to do great things.

Because once you have that ikigai in focus, it's time to start building the skills that will help you bring it to life.

4

UNITE WITH UNIQUELY HUMAN SKILLS

Why are human skills more essential than technical skills? Exhibit A took place 15 years before ChatGPT ever launched...

It was January 9, 2007.

As you may know, that was the day that Steve Jobs walked onto the Macworld stage to introduce the iPhone.

But here's what you may not know: On January 9, 2007, every other major company was already building *technically superior* smartphones. BlackBerry had world-class email integration. Windows Mobile had the most features. Palm had better stylus technology.

The technical specs weren't even close.

And so Jobs didn't spend 90 minutes listing processor speeds, memory configurations, and network protocols.

Instead, he told a story:

"Today, we're introducing three revolutionary products. A widescreen iPod with touch controls. A revolutionary mobile phone. And a breakthrough internet communications device."

He paused. Let it sink in.

"An iPod, a phone, an internet communicator. An iPod, a phone... Are you getting it?"

Another pause. The audience started to murmur.

"These are not three separate devices. This is *one device*. And we are calling it iPhone."

The audience erupted.

Not because of the technology. But because Jobs had just redefined what a phone *could be*. He understood what people truly wanted (seamless experiences, not feature lists), engaged them through masterful storytelling, and led them to envision a completely new future of computing.

The result? The iPhone became the most valuable product in business history, generating over $1 trillion in revenue. Not because it was technically superior, but because Jobs possessed something his engineering-focused competitors lacked: the complete mastery of human skills that no algorithm could replicate.

THE HUMAN SKILLS HIERARCHY: YOUR CAREER INSURANCE POLICY

Jobs' success wasn't accidental - it followed a precise hierarchy that research now shows is directly correlated with earning potential and career resilience in the AI age:

- **Level 1: Understanding Humans** - Jobs recognized that people wanted elegant experiences, not technical feature lists
- **Level 2: Engaging Humans** - His theatrical presentation made dry technical achievements feel magical and alluring
- **Level 3: Leading Humans** - Ultimately, he transformed how humanity thought about mobile computing - from a gimmicky sideshow to the main attraction

Each level builds on the previous one, and each level correlates directly with earning potential and job security. Here's why:

Research shows that 85% of job success comes from people skills, yet we spend 72% of our professional development budgets on technical skills.[31] We're optimizing for the wrong thing entirely.

While AI rapidly masters technical capabilities, it fundamentally cannot replicate human consciousness, emotion, or social intuition. This creates a "complementary scarcity" - as AI gets better at technical tasks, human skills become exponentially more valuable.

So the clear path forward is to double down on those human skills, just like Jobs bet the company on a humanistic - not technical -

---

31 "The Soft Skills Disconnect," National Soft Skills Organization, April 22, 2025, https://www.nationalsoftskills.org/the-soft-skills-disconnect.

vision of the future. And to do so, it helps to understand each of these essential skillsets in depth.

LEVEL 1:
UNDERSTANDING HUMANS

In 1979, a 26-year-old industrial designer named Patricia Moore walked into a meeting at Raymond Loewy's prestigious New York firm with a simple suggestion: What if we designed products that elderly people could actually use?

The men in the room laughed. One told her bluntly: "We don't design for *those* people."

The Three-Year Undercover Mission

Moore's response? For the next three years, she traveled to 116 cities throughout North America disguised as an elderly woman.

She wore clouded contact lenses to simulate vision loss. Taped her fingers together to mimic arthritis. Used splints, bandages, and corsets to alter her posture.

Simple tasks became ordeals: Riding buses. Zipping zippers. Stepping off a curb. All "tiring, debilitating, and devastating," as she later described them.

But the physical challenges were only half the story. The invisibility was worse.

"Not until I went into character did I feel that anger, that anxiety, and sense of worthlessness that can come from just coping with the environment." She heard elderly women apologize through tears about incontinence. She experienced being ignored, rushed, dismissed as less-than-human.[32]

When Understanding Becomes Revolutionary

Moore emerged with a fury-driven mission: to destroy what she called "Darwinian design" - products designed so that "only the fit can use them."

She started her own firm and revolutionized product design for Kimberly-Clark, Merck, Johnson & Johnson, and OXO. She helped develop Depend undergarments, redesigned medicine containers with universal symbols, and championed "universal design" - the philosophy that good design works for everyone.

In 2019, she received the Cooper Hewitt Smithsonian Design Museum's National Design Award.[33]

Patricia Moore didn't just *feel* empathy for the elderly. She lived their reality for three years, absorbed their systematic invisibility, and then weaponized that understanding into products that transformed an entire industry.

That's not "soft" skills. That's revolutionary.

---

32 "26-Year-Old Sleuth's Transformation Brings Elderly's Obstacles into Focus," *Chicago Tribune*, August 18, 1985, https://www.chicagotribune. com/1985/08/18/26-year-old-sleuths-transformation-brings-elderlys-obstacles/.

33 Cooper Hewitt, Smithsonian Design Museum. "2019 National Design Award Winners." Accessed October 6, 2025. https://www.cooperhewitt. org/national-design-awards/2019-national-design-awards-winners/.

The ROI of Understanding

This is the same foundation Jobs built when he understood that people didn't want better phones - they wanted better experiences.

And the business case for understanding your customers is off the charts. For instance, a University of Cambridge study found that for every one-point increase in salespeople's empathy ratings (on a 5-point scale), they drove 10% more sales.[34]

Why? Because in a world with endless choice, why do business with a robotic, AI-like salesperson when you can work with someone who actually understands you?

What AI Can't Do

Here's the neural science behind empathy's ROI: When you truly listen to someone - not just hear their words, but absorb their emotions - your brain's mirror neurons fire in patterns that literally simulate their experience.[35]

You're not just processing information, you're imagining yourself in their shoes. Which is the very thing that AI *can't* do.

Because yes, AI can analyze sentiment. It can process feedback. It can predict behavior.

---

34 Prabhu, Jaideep, and colleagues. *"Does Empathy Improve Marketing Performance? The Role of Cognitive and Emotional Empathy in Sales."* Working paper, Cambridge Judge Business School, 2017. https://www.jbs.cam.ac.uk/wp-content/uploads/2020/08/currentresearch-empathy-prabhu.pdf

35 Iacoboni, M. (2009). "Imitation, Empathy, and Mirror Neurons." *Annual Review of Psychology*, 60, 653-670. https://www.annualreviews.org/doi/10.1146/annurev.psych.60.110707.163604

But AI doesn't have a body that ages. It's never felt the shame of incontinence or the invisibility of being dismissed. It's never experienced arthritic fingers struggling with a zipper.

Which means that AI can process the *data* of human experience. But only humans can *understand* it.

And that understanding? It's the foundation everything else builds on.

Because you can't engage people you don't understand. And you certainly can't influence or lead people you haven't first learned to see.

LEVEL 2: ENGAGING HUMANS

So understanding people is the first step. But understanding alone doesn't change anything.

You need to actually move people. To inspire action. To make them *feel* something so deeply that doing nothing becomes impossible.

And here's the thing AI struggles with: While machines can analyze what people want, only humans can make them *care*.

Let me show you what I mean.

When Data Met Reality

Melinda French Gates had a problem.

It was 2012, and her team at the Gates Foundation had killer data: Spreadsheets proving that family planning could save thousands of lives. Economic models showing massive returns on investment. The kind of analysis that should make any rational decision-maker whip out their checkbook.

And yet? World leaders weren't budging.

So Gates did something different. She flew to Koira Tegui, Niger - one of the hottest places on Earth - to see what was actually happening on the ground.

There, she met Sadi Seyni.

Seyni had walked six miles in 104°F heat to reach a family planning clinic. She risked a beating from her husband to make the journey. Why? "Another baby could kill me and the children I have."

When Seyni finally arrived at the clinic, they turned her away. Out of stock.

The Strategy Shift
That Changed Everything

Gates returned from Niger and completely abandoned her spreadsheet strategy.

In donor meetings leading up to the London Summit on Family Planning, she didn't lead with cost-benefit analyses or economic projections. She told Seyni's story.

And on stage at the Summit, Gates did something radical. She replaced the usual pie charts with a single photo: the clinic's empty chair. Then she asked one simple question:

"Will we let her walk home again with nothing?"

The result? The summit didn't just hit its goals. It *shattered* them. $4.6 billion raised. Commitments from 20 nations to expand contraceptive access.[36]

That single story unlocked billions in funding that no cost-benefit analysis could touch.

Not because the data wasn't compelling. But because stories engage neural networks that facts simply cannot reach.

Your Brain on Stories

Here's what's actually happening in your brain right now as you read about Seyni's six-mile walk:

Neuroscientists have discovered a phenomenon called "neural coupling."[37] When you're truly engaged by a story, your brain waves start to mirror the storyteller's. Researchers using fMRI scans found that listeners' brains don't just passively receive information - they synchronize with the speaker's brain patterns.

In other words, storytelling is the closest thing we have to a Vulcan Mind Meld outside of *Star Trek*.

Think about what that means. When Gates told Seyni's story, she wasn't just conveying information. She was literally making donors *feel* what she felt standing in that clinic. Their neurons fired in patterns that mirrored her experience of outrage, empathy, and moral urgency.

---

36 Gates, Melinda. *The Moment of Lift: How Empowering Women Changes the World*. New York: Flatiron Books, 2019.

37 Stephens, G. J., Silbert, L. J., & Hasson, U. (2010). "Speaker–listener neural coupling underlies successful communication." *Proceedings of the National Academy of Sciences*, 107(32), 14425-14430. https://doi.org/10.1073/pnas.1008662107

The $3,600 Thrift Store Experiment

Still think stories are just for kids? Let me hit you with some cold, hard ROI.

Researchers Rob Walker and Joshua Glenn ran an experiment to see if they could put an exact pricetag on the power of storytelling.[38] Here's what they did:

1. Bought 100 cheap trinkets at thrift stores for a total of $128.74
2. Commissioned 100 authors to write stories about these objects
3. Listed them on eBay with the stories as product descriptions

The result? Those thrift store trinkets sold for $3,612.51.

That's a **2,706% increase in value.** From stories alone.

Same objects. Same platform. The only difference? Human storytelling transformed literal junk into treasures people wanted to own.

Can ChatGPT turn $129 worth of garage sale leftovers into $3,600? Not a chance. Because what sold wasn't the objects - it was the *meaning* humans created around them.

---

38 Walker, R., & Glenn, J. (2012). *Significant Objects: 100 Extraordinary Stories About Ordinary Things*. Fantagraphics Books. See also: https://significantobjects.com/

LEVEL 3: LEADING HUMANS

Of all our human skills, leadership is where the gap between human and machine becomes a chasm.

Why? Because leadership requires something machines fundamentally lack: the ability to make people believe in futures that don't exist yet. To inspire others to risk everything for an idea. To create meaning in the face of mortality.

Don't believe me? Let's wind the tape back just a few years...

When a Comedian Became a Wartime Legend

It's February 2022. Russian tanks are rolling toward Kyiv. The Ukrainian president - a former TV comedian named Volodymyr Zelensky - is about to make a decision that would change history.

The smart move is obvious. Every advisor, every ally, every expert says the same thing: Get out. Establish a government-in-exile. Live to fight another day. The U.S. has evacuation plans ready.

Zelensky's response? *"I need ammunition, not a ride."*

Within 48 hours of that legendary stand:

- Germany reversed a decades-long policy against sending weapons into conflict zones
- The European Union announced it would supply fighter jets for the first time in its history

- Even famously neutral Switzerland froze Russian assets, abandoning a position it had held through two world wars[39]

Why? Because Zelensky didn't just refuse evacuation. He transformed himself from a politician into a symbol. He embodied the vision he sought for his nation.

That's leadership. Not strategy. Not tactics. But *willing* the future into existence.

The Neuroscience of Leadership

Here's what's actually happening in people's brains when they encounter great leadership: Research shows that inspirational leadership activates the brain's reward circuitry and releases oxytocin - the neurochemical responsible for trust and bonding.[40]

This is why Zelensky's physical presence in Kyiv mattered more than any speech from safety ever could. His actions triggered the biological mechanisms that transform scattered individuals into unified groups willing to take massive risks.

And no, AI can't replicate this. Because AI doesn't have a body to put on the line. It doesn't have mortality to transcend. So it can't create meaning in the same deep, visceral way a great human leader can.

---

39 "Policy Shift: Berlin to Deliver Defensive Weapons to Ukraine," *Reuters*, February 26, 2022, https://www.reuters.com/world/europe/policy-shift-berlin-approve-export-rpgs-kyiv-by-third-country-2022-02-26

40 Zak, P. J. (2017). "The Neuroscience of Trust." *Harvard Business Review*. https://hbr.org/2017/01/the-neuroscience-of-trust

The Numbers Don't Lie

The performance gap here is massive. Research from leadership development firm Zenger Folkman tracked leaders at a large financial services company and found something stunning: Great leaders generated $4.5 million in revenue per office managed. Poor leaders? They *lost* $1.2 million.[41]

What can explain this huge chasm in outcomes?

It turns out that the best leaders had 57% of their employees highly committed to the organization, while the worst leaders managed only 11% commitment. Which means, just like Zelensky, they were able to activate way more human talent than less-effective leaders.

Because great leaders don't just make people feel good - they activate the human desire for meaning and progress that translates into real-world results.

BUILDING YOUR
HUMAN SKILLS ARSENAL

Alright, remember that ikigai you identified in Chapter 3? That sweet spot where your strengths, passions, market demand, and AI-resistance all intersect?

Time to do something with it.

Not in five years. Not when you're "ready." Now.

---

41 "How Extraordinary Leaders Double Profits," April 27, 2019, https:// zengerfolkman.com/leadership-studies/how-extraordinary-leaders-double-profits/.

Because here's the dirty secret about human skills: You can't learn empathy from a book. You can't master storytelling in a workshop. And you definitely can't develop leadership by watching TED talks.

You learn these skills the same way Patricia Moore, Melinda Gates, and Zelensky did: By doing something real, with real stakes, where real people are counting on you.

So we're going to snag a 2-for-1 deal right now:

1. Create a side project that develops domain skills in your chosen field…
2. …While also building the very human skills that make you AI-proof

And we're going to do it in just four weeks.

Your 4-Week Side Project: The Ultimate Human Skills Bootcamp

Here's what you're going to build: A micro-entrepreneurial project in your ikigai space.

Now, before you freak out - this isn't about quitting your job or becoming the next Bill Gates. This is about creating something small enough to manage alongside your current life, but real enough that it forces you to develop genuinely useful skills.

Think:

- A consulting service with a first client
- A workshop or course with 10 students
- A community or newsletter with 100 subscribers

The exact format doesn't matter. What matters is that you're creating something that requires you to:

- **Understand humans** (by talking to potential customers about their real problems)
- **Engage humans** (by telling a story compelling enough that they pay attention)
- **Lead humans** (by inspiring them to become your first customers)

Let's start with Week 1:

Week 1: Define Your Micro-Project

First, you need to pick what you're actually building.

Use this prompt to brainstorm:

 PROMPT

I'd like to build up my human skills in [my target role/industry].

Generate 10 micro-entrepreneurial projects I could launch in 4 weeks that:

1. Are relevant to my desired role and industry

2. Will require me to understand my audience, engage them with compelling stories,
and lead them to take action
3. Can start with zero budget

For each project, list the target audience
and the problem I'm solving.

Here's an example for an aspiring Data Analyst who's passionate
about sustainability:

 **AI OUTPUT**

1. "The Data Clarity Project" –
Making Complex Insights Understandable

Goal:
Take confusing public data (e.g., government, climate, education) and turn it into
clear, relatable visuals or stories.

⊚ **Target Audience:**

- Everyday professionals and students
  who want to understand data-driven
  news.

💡 **Problem Solved:**

- People feel overwhelmed or alien-
  ated by data-heavy information; you
  translate complexity into clarity
  and insight.

> **Why it matters:**
> You practice simplifying data for real audiences — a critical analyst skill in business settings.

Even if you're just starting out in a new field, there's always a great way to cut your teeth!

Alternatively, if you're trying to break into EdTech Marketing, you might build a YouTube channel where you interview teachers about their biggest technology challenges.

Or if you're looking to level up as a senior leader in Mechanical Engineering, perhaps you start a Substack where you share expertise about building and leading teams.

No matter what, pick the idea that excites you most AND scares you a little. Because if it doesn't scare you just a bit, it's probably not ambitious enough to force real growth.

Week 2: Understand Your Audience

Remember how Patricia Moore spent three years living as an elderly person? You're going to do something similar - just *way more* compressed.

Your mission: Interview **three** people you want to serve.

And don't worry if you don't know these people yet. You can find them with this prompt:

PROMPT

I'm looking for [Target Audience] who might face [Problem You're Solving].

Help me find the following groups:

- 5 specific LinkedIn groups where my audience hangs out
- 5 specific subreddits related to their problem
- 5 Facebook groups they're likely in

Here's what that might look like that for our sustainability-focused Data Analyst:

AI OUTPUT

Here's a curated list of online communities where people interested in sustainability (and who may struggle with dense climate science) hang out. You can join these to listen, engage, and share value.

🔗 **5 LinkedIn Groups**

1. **"Sustainability and Circularity LinkedIn Groups"** –
   - A collective reference to groups on energy, waste, recycling, green building, etc.

2. **"Sustainability Reporting Professionals Group"** –

- Focused on professionals reporting ESG / sustainability impact.

3. **"Leaders in Sustainability Network"**
   –

   - Private community of sustainability leaders, advisors, and certification partners.

Don't just look for an audience one-by-one - that's too slow.
Find out where they hang out - and go directly to them!

Once you've got the groups, you can make a post like the following:

 Hey all!

I'm working on a project to help [target audience] with [problem], and I'm trying to make sure I actually understand the challenge before building anything.

Would you be willing to chat for 10 minutes about your experience with [topic]? I'm not selling anything - just would love to learn from your experience.

Thanks for considering!

[your name]

And then you can kick-off your interviews with juicy questions like these:

1. What's the biggest challenge with [the problem you're looking to solve]?
2. What would make that challenge a lot easier for you?
3. If you had a magic wand and could make this problem disappear, how would that make things better?

At the end of these interviews, you'll not only have built-up your Understanding skills - you'll also have a way better foundation for telling your story in Week 3!

Week 3: Engage Your Audience

This is your Melinda Gates week. So just like Melinda, you're going to transform what you learned into a story so compelling that strangers pay attention.

Specifically, you're going to create a powerful **3-minute** *video* **story** because that forces you to:

- Distill your message to what actually matters
- Practice your delivery and authentic presence
- Develop the storytelling skills that AI can't replicate

Start by developing a three-act script, just like the one Melinda Gates used in London:

ACT 1 - THE PROBLEM (1 minute)

Open with a specific story from your experience or your interviews:

"Meet [Name]. [Describe their specific struggle in vivid detail]. Unfortunately, this is all too common since I heard the same themes from others in the community."

ACT 2 - THE SOLUTION (1 minute)

Pivot to what you want to build out:

"But it doesn't have to be this way. Here's what we can actually do about it: [Describe your solution]."

ACT 3 - THE CALL TO ACTION (1 minute)

"So if you'd like to learn more, [take this specific action]. I'm confident that, together, we can make a big dent in achieving [the benefits of the solution]."

Note two things about this script-writing process:

1. You don't want AI to write the script for you since *you* want to build your Engagement muscles - not just outsource that skill to a chatbot.

2. But it doesn't have to be painful. Because you've already done the hard work of learning from your audience, you can paste those visceral details right into the script for instant engagement.

The end result should be something like this - again, drawing upon our Data Analyst example:

> Meet Nate. He sits on his town's Sustainability Taskforce. He leads a big tree-planting effort every Arbor Day. And he always, always recycles. But the one thing Nate doesn't do is have any clue what the latest environmental research means for his community or himself. As Nate told me, "I'm an insurance salesman, not a scientist!" And Nate's not alone - 75% of all Americans report not being aware of the latest environmental findings.
>
> But it doesn't have to be this way. What if there was a really simple way to visualize complicated environmental data? And figure out exactly how to put that data to work in your life and community? This kind of Citizen's Guide to Environmental Research is exactly what I'd like to build.
>
> So what do you say? If you're like Nate and want to stay on top of the latest research - without getting a PhD in Environmental Science - just let me know in the Comments. I'd be happy to keep you updated on this project so we can all understand our planet just a little better!

With your script in hand, it's time to record your video. And don't worry about stuff that doesn't matter (fancy cameras, lighting, etc.). Just start with your phone or webcam because there are really just three elements to great delivery:

1. *Can people understand you?* Speak clearly and confidently.

2. *Can people identify with you?* Speak naturally, just like you would to a friend across the table.

3. *Can people get excited by you?* Speak with the kind of emotion that reflects the power of the problem and solution.

Finally, before you share your video with the community, use AI for what it's really good for - not telling your story, but taking your story to the next level. Here's how to test your video with a feedback-focused prompt:

PROMPT

Review the attached video and tell me:

1. Is my opening engaging and compelling?
2. Is my solution clear and logical?
3. Is my call to action motivating and persuasive?

For anything that falls short of these goals, please suggest tweaks to enhance the efficacy of my storytelling.

Here's what that might look like for the Data Analytics project:

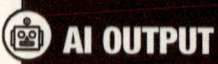 **AI OUTPUT**

This is a thoughtful pitch that clearly defines a problem and proposes a valuable solution. The use of a relatable character ("Nate") is a great storytelling technique!

Here is my breakdown of your video against your goals, along with suggestions tailored to your expertise in helping career coaches leverage AI and LinkedIn (as your content could be great material for them to share with students).

1. Is my opening engaging and compelling?

Assessment: Yes, the opening is very effective due to the character-driven hook.
The introduction of **Nate** personalizes an abstract problem (lack of environmental awareness). You quickly establish his credentials (Task Force, tree planting, recycling) before delivering the punchline: he's still unaware of the key research. The statistic following Nate's story logically validates that his problem is widespread.
...

AI is actually a much better critic than it is a
writer. So use that superpower wisely!

Just keep in mind that not every chatbot can handle video. So you may want to turn to Gemini on this one since that's one of its particular superpowers.

And then, after making any final revisions, be sure to share your video with the original communities to get the ultimate skill-building feedback - i.e., feedback from actual humans!

Week 4: Lead Your Audience

Understanding your audience got you research. Engaging them got you attention.

Now, just like Volodymyr Zelensky, it's time to lead them. And, just like Zelensky, there has to be skin in the game - something to ask of your audience that's more than just a Like or a Comment.

So start by brainstorming your Ask with a prompt like the following:

PROMPT

I'm building [describe your project] to help [describe your audience] [describe the problem you're solving].

What are 10 small but meaningful commitments I can ask of my audience so they have some skin in the game?

🤖 AI OUTPUT

That's a great way to frame it — **"small but meaningful commitments"** give your readers a sense of personal stake while reinforcing the data-driven mindset at the core of your Citizen's Guide.

Here are **10 thoughtfully designed commitments** that combine personal action, observation, and data literacy:

1. Measure One Thing in Your Own Life
Ask readers to pick one environmental variable — home energy use, miles traveled, food waste, etc. — and track it for a month.

"What gets measured gets understood."

They'll experience firsthand how data reveals patterns they'd otherwise miss.

Sometimes the hardest part of getting started is just knowing what to ask for. That's the perfect time to turn to AI to put some ideas on the table!

Note that the Ask could be financial (e.g., pay $10 to subscribe to my Substack), but it doesn't have to. Instead, you could ask for a commitment of time, action, and/or energy.

The bottom line is that you just want to make sure you're asking for something real and valuable, since that's the ultimate test of leadership.

And then, once you've got your Ask fine-tuned, it's time to make it. So here's a recipe you can use to set it up:

STEP 1 - START WITH VISION

Before you get into all the juicy details, be sure to set the stage:

"Imagine a world where [describe the end goal of your work]."

STEP 2 - MAKE THE ASK

But don't get too caught up in the hypotheticals - make sure to ground them in the specific request:

"Here's how we get there. I'm building [describe your project] to tackle this challenge and I need your help. Specifically, I'm looking for people who are willing to step up by [describe your request]."

STEP 3 - SELL THE RESULTS

Be sure to bring everything back to what your audience actually cares about:

"With your help, I'm confident that we can [describe your end goal]. So [describe the specific action required] today."

Here's what this would look like in a post for the Sustainability Data project:

> What if it was way easier to connect the dots between environmental research and actions you can take in your own community?
>
> That's exactly what I'm building with my Citizen's Guide to Environmental Research - but I need your help. Specifically, I need people who are willing to commit to tracking their home energy use for 30 days.
>
> With the data you gather, we'll be able to validate energy efficiency research at the local level, paving the way for way more communities to take these steps. All you need to do is sign-up on my Google Form and I'll send you next steps right away.

Be sure to share your post in all of your original communities, with everyone who expressed interest in your video, and, of course, all the amazing folks you interviewed at the very beginning. Your goal is to capitalize on all the goodwill you built up in the last few weeks and convert it into the most important human resource of all: Action!

What You've Actually Built

Before we get into the details of building out your project (which we'll bring to life with the aid of AI tools in the next chapter), let's just reflect back on the progress you made in the past four weeks.

First of all, you didn't just "learn about" human skills. You developed them:

- **Level 1 - Understanding Humans:** You conducted interviews with the very people you need to understand the most. Many professionals have never spoken to the end users of their products/services at all!
- **Level 2 - Engaging Humans:** You crafted a story compelling enough to make strangers care. Many people are afraid to even put themselves out there, let alone motivate others.
- **Level 3 - Leading Humans:** You inspired people to take action. Very few people ever take on the mantle of leadership.

But even more important than all of those skills, here's what you really built: **Proof.**

Proof that you can:

- Identify unmet needs in your target audience
- Create something people value
- Navigate ambiguity and setbacks
- Lead without authority
- Create value from nothing

You know what that's called? **Agency.**

The ability to create value independent of a job title, a manager's approval, or a company's resources. And the very thing that's in short supply in a world that's more and more reliant upon AI.

Which means that, when you walk into your next job interview, you won't just show up like everyone else with a list of previous job titles.

You'll show up with a story:

> "I'm so excited about applying data analytics to sustainability that I even built an entire project in this space. I started by interviewing regular people who wanted to know more about climate science, channeled their desires into a Citizen's Guide to Environmental Research, and led 100 community members to create their very own experiment that validated international studies in their local context. Which is why I'd love to help this organization do the same thing - just on a 1,000X scale..."

Think about what this signals:

- **Initiative** (didn't wait for permission)
- **Customer obsession** (did actual research)
- **Storytelling** (can engage people)
- **Leadership** (got people to follow)
- **Results** (actual outcomes)

While everyone else says "I'm a hard worker and team player," you're showing receipts.

Failure > Not Showing Up

But what if your project failed?

What if you only got 2 customers instead of 10, or made $0, or realized your idea has no legs at all?

Guess what? **You still win.**

Because just like Moore and Gates and Zelensky, you showed up. And you built the human skills that don't just matter today, but will matter even more *tomorrow*.

That's because, unlike technical skills that rapidly become obsolete no matter how widely used today, human skills are becoming MORE valuable as they become scarcer and scarcer.

But just to be clear: Future success isn't about human skills vs. AI skills. It's about both skillsets paired together for massive potential.

So if you're ready to leverage your newfound human skills with the very best of AI - and to build out your new project in powerful ways - read on to the next chapter!

5

REINFORCE WITH RELEVANT AI

Picture this: It's 2007, and Netflix is burning through cash. They're spending $300 million annually shipping DVDs in red envelopes while Blockbuster dominates with 60,000 employees and 9,000 stores worldwide.

Netflix has two choices: Use technology to make DVD shipping more efficient (e.g., build robots to stuff envelopes faster), or use technology to fundamentally change how the entertainment industry works.

They choose transformation over automation.

Instead of optimizing their logistics, Netflix builds recommendation algorithms that analyze viewing patterns to predict what users want to watch next. But more importantly, they use this technology foundation to completely reinvent content delivery - moving from physical DVDs to streaming, creating original content, and building a global entertainment ecosystem. They don't just digitize their existing business; they create an entirely new business.[42]

The result? Netflix becomes a $500 billion streaming giant while Blockbuster files for bankruptcy.[43]

All because of a simple choice between two technology strategies: One focused on doing the same work faster, the other on doing fundamentally better work.

And that choice? It's the exact same one you're making with AI right now.

LIGHTING $40 BILLION ON FIRE: WHY 95% OF AI EFFORTS FAIL

Here's a statistic that should terrify every CIO: MIT research shows that 95% of AI pilots in Fortune 500 companies fail to deliver measurable ROI. Companies are spending between $30-40 billion annually on enterprise AI initiatives, and the vast majority is producing zero financial return.[44]

Why the spectacular failure rate?

Because most companies - and most professionals - are making the same fundamental mistake that Netflix almost made: They're

---

42 "How Netflix's Recommendations System Works," Netflix TechBlog, April 6, 2006, https://netflixtechblog.com/netflix-recommendations-beyond-the-5-stars-part-1-55838468f429.

43 "Netflix Market Cap 2010-2025," Macrotrends, accessed October 26, 2025, https://www.macrotrends.net/stocks/charts/NFLX/netflix/market-cap; "Blockbuster Files for Bankruptcy," *The New York Times*, September 23, 2010, https://www.nytimes.com/2010/09/24/business/24blockbuster.html.

44 "MIT Report Finds 95% of Generative AI Pilots Fail to Deliver Financial Impact," AInvest, August 18, 2025, https://www.ainvest.com/news/mit-report-finds-95-generative-ai-pilots-fail-deliver-financial-impact-2508/.

trying to use technology to do their existing work faster, rather than to do fundamentally better work.

Specifically, they're slapping AI onto existing processes and expecting magic. "Let's use AI to write our emails!" "Let's use AI to generate our reports!" "Let's use AI to analyze our data!"

But the problem isn't the technology. Instead, as the research authors point out, the real issue is the "learning gap" between what we naively assume AI is good at vs. its true capabilities.[45]

THE PRODUCTIVITY PARADOX: THE ILLUSION DRIVING THE FAILURES

To understand what's driving this learning gap, let's consider another research project that dove even deeper into how we misunderstand AI.

A 2025 study by METR (Model Evaluation & Threat Research) tracked 16 experienced software developers working on their own open-source projects, using the most advanced AI coding models available.

Before starting, researchers asked: "How much faster do you think AI will make you?"

The developers' prediction: "About 24% faster."

After completing 246 real-world coding tasks, researchers asked again: "How much faster did AI make you?"

---

45 "MIT report: 95% of generative AI pilots at companies are failing," *Fortune*, August 18, 2025, https://fortune.com/2025/08/18/mit-report-95-percent-generative-ai-pilots-at-companies-failing-cfo/.

The developers' answer: "About 20% faster."

Then the researchers measured the actual time from start to finish.

The reality? The developers were actually 19% *slower*.[46]

But here's the truly alarming part: Even after being shown the data proving they were slower, the developers *still believed* AI had sped them up by 20%. The gap between perception and reality was a staggering 39 percentage points.

This is exactly what's happening in those failed enterprise AI pilots. Leaders feel productive. Teams report time savings. Everyone believes the AI initiative is working. But the actual business results - the ROI - never materialize.

Why does this massive disconnect exist?

Because AI creates what researchers call "the illusion of productivity." When you type a prompt and code instantly appears on your screen, your brain releases dopamine. That instant feedback *feels* like progress. The editor is buzzing with activity. Lines of code are appearing. You're *doing something*.

But as the METR researchers noted, "dopamine rewards activity in the editor, not working code in production."

The developers *felt* productive because they were *doing more stuff*. But that stuff didn't actually result in shipping better code faster. Instead, they spent their time:

- Prompting the AI and waiting for responses
- Reviewing AI-generated code for errors

---

46 Joel Becker and Nate Thomas, "Measuring the Impact of Early-2025 AI on Experienced Open-Source Developer Productivity," METR, July 10, 2025, https://metr.org/blog/2025-07-10-early-2025-ai-experienced-os-dev-study/.

- Debugging subtle mistakes that looked correct at first glance
- Going back to correct problems that wouldn't have existed if they'd just written the code themselves

In other words, they were working harder to clean up AI's mess than they would have worked to just do it right the first time.

THE DARKEST SIDE OF SUBSTITUTION: THE SKILL DEATH SPIRAL

What these developers and firms are experiencing is the dark side of using AI for "Substitution."

Substitution is when you use AI to replace your thinking. To take over your tasks. To do your work *for* you.

And it fails not just because of the illusion of productivity but because of what researchers at MIT Media Lab call **"cognitive debt"** - the hidden cost you pay when relying on AI makes it harder to build and maintain your own thinking skills.[47]

Here's what that looks like in practice:

The researchers tracked 54 college students over four months as they wrote essays. They divided students into three groups: one used ChatGPT, one used traditional search engines, and one wrote without any tools.

---

47 Kosmyna, N., Hauptmann, E., Yuan, Y. T., Situ, J., Liao, X-H., Beresnitzky, A. V., Braunstein, I., & Maes, P. (2025). "Your Brain on ChatGPT: Accumulation of Cognitive Debt when Using an AI Assistant for Essay Writing Task." arXiv preprint arXiv:2506.08872, https://arxiv.org/abs/2506.08872.

The results were startling.

The students who relied on ChatGPT showed measurably weaker brain connectivity patterns. Using EEG to monitor brain activity, researchers found that "brain connectivity systematically scaled down with the amount of external support" - meaning the more students relied on AI, the less their brains actually engaged with the work.

But here's where it gets truly concerning: When researchers switched the ChatGPT users to writing without any tools in the fourth session, these students were no longer able to engage at the level of students who'd been writing independently all along.

The AI had atrophied their cognitive muscles.

And the students didn't even realize it was happening. They reported high satisfaction with their AI-assisted work. They felt productive. But when asked to quote a sentence from their own essays, ChatGPT users couldn't do it - because, of course, they hadn't actually processed what they'd "written."

This is the substitution death spiral:

1. **AI does your work** → You feel productive and satisfied
2. **Your brain engagement drops** → You don't notice because the output looks good
3. **Your cognitive skills atrophy** → The neural pathways that build expertise weaken
4. **You become dependent** → When AI is removed, you can't perform at your previous level

And it doesn't just affect college students writing arbitrary essays. Research from Carnegie Mellon and Microsoft found the exact same pattern with knowledge workers: The more confident workers were in AI's ability to complete tasks, the less they leveraged their own critical thinking. As one researcher noted, this creates "a key irony of automation" - by letting AI handle routine tasks, "you deprive the user of the routine opportunities to practice their judgment and strengthen their cognitive musculature, leaving them atrophied."[48]

THE AMPLIFICATION ALTERNATIVE: BUILDING SKILLS, NOT ERODING THEM

Before you give up on AI as an insidious waster of both time and skills, consider this: There's a way to use AI that doesn't just avoid skill atrophy - it actually builds those cognitive muscles stronger than ever.

Remember those MIT students whose brains disengaged when they used ChatGPT? The same study found something remarkable about the students who used search engines: Their brain connectivity patterns remained strong. In fact, they showed higher engagement than students working without any tools at all.[49]

Why? Because search required them to think. They had to:

- Formulate good questions
- Evaluate sources critically

---

48   Lee, M. K., Park, J. S., & Zimmerman, J. (2025). "The Impact of Generative AI on Critical Thinking: Self-Reported Experiences of Knowledge Workers." CHI '25: Proceedings of the 2025 CHI Conference on Human Factors in Computing Systems, https://www.microsoft.com/en-us/research/wp-content/uploads/2025/01/lee_2025_ai_critical_thinking_survey.pdf.

49   Kosmyna et al., "Your Brain on ChatGPT."

- Synthesize information from multiple places
- Make judgments about what mattered
- Construct their own arguments

The tool expanded what they could access, but they maintained control over the thinking.

That's Amplification.

And it's not about using different tools - it's about using AI strategically, with a framework that ensures you're building skills rather than outsourcing them.

Think back to Netflix at the beginning of this chapter. They didn't use technology to stuff envelopes faster (substitution). They used it to completely reimagine how people discover and consume content (amplification).

Here's the difference in practice:

Substitution:

AI writes your email → It feels good so let AI write your next email → Your writing skills start to atrophy → Each new email becomes harder to write on your own → You become dependent on AI → Your unique value decreases

Amplification:

You draft your own emails → AI provides feedback → You sharpen your writing skills → You write more because you feel more confident → Your skill development starts to compound → Your unique value increases

Substitution:

AI analyzes your data and tells you what it means → You report the findings and get immediate praise → You let AI analyze data next time → Your analytical skills atrophy → Your boss discovers that AI is actually better at doing your job than you are → You need to look for a new job

Amplification:

You use AI to analyze a qualitative dataset that would have been impossible to crystallize before → You identify connections between this data and your company's key goals → Your boss is so impressed she gives you bigger challenges than before → Your analytical and presentation skills grow → You get a promotion

See the pattern?

Substitution:

AI does your job today → You enjoy success in the short term → Your skills atrophy in the medium term → Your career declines in the long term

Amplification:

You use AI to make you better at what needs to get done today → It's more challenging in the short term → Your skills grow in the medium term → Your career soars in the long term

THE AMPLIFICATION FRAMEWORK

Here's what most people get wrong: They think amplification is just about using AI "the right way."

It's not.

Amplification requires a systematic framework. Because without strategy, you'll drift back into substitution without even realizing it. Those developers and students *thought* they were using AI correctly. They felt fast, they felt productive. But they were actually making themselves slower and weaker.

To avoid that trap, here's your three stage blueprint:

Phase 1: Set a Clear Goal
Not "use AI to save time."
Not "be more productive."
But: *What specific outcome is most important to you, regardless of AI?*

Example: "My #1 goal is to close more deals this quarter than last."

Notice the difference? This goal is about achieving a better *outcome* (driving revenue, the company's lifeblood), not just a faster *process* (getting through lead research more quickly).

Phase 2: Identify Your Pareto Drivers
Not "what takes the most time."
Not "what I don't like doing."
But: *What 20% of activities drive 80% of your results toward that goal?*

Example: "The #1 predictor of whether a deal closes is whether the lead matches the ideal customer profile established by existing customers. On the other hand, the following things have little bearing on our ultimate success even though we spend a lot of time on them: Emails, Website Visits, and Discounts."

I know this is hard. The Pareto Principle (i.e., the 80/20 Rule) inevitably involves sacrificing some sacred cows. And yet future-proofing your career requires ruthless focus on prioritization, so take a deep breath and then focus on what matters.

Phase 3: Amplify with AI

Not "have AI do my job for me."

Not "automate everything."

But: *How can AI amplify those high-impact activities without replacing your unique judgment?*

Example: "Use AI to review our customer database and identify the key factors that correlate with customer buying - and then have it scan our CRM to identify the most promising prospects that fit that model. But instead of having AI send generic emails to all these prospects, I use my own sales expertise to deliver highly customized outreach. So AI handles volume. I provide human judgment."

This is the crucial distinction: AI expands your capacity to do high-value work, but you maintain control over the thinking that matters most.

Without all three phases, you'll fall back into substitution. You'll optimize for feeling productive instead of being effective. You'll join the 95% who waste their AI investment.

But with this framework? You'll join the 5% who are using AI to become exponentially more capable, not just fractionally faster. Who are using AI to do work at a level that wasn't possible before.

Let me show you exactly how this works with a real example of someone who got it right - and in doing so, literally saved lives.

THE DOCTOR WHO LEARNED TO DANCE WITH AI

It's 3:47 AM on a Saturday night in the emergency room, and Dr. Harvey Castro is seeing his 47th patient of the shift.

She's a 52-year-old woman with chest pain. Vital signs are mostly stable. She's describing a burning sensation that gets worse after eating. Classic presentation for gastroesophageal reflux disease—GERD. Probably ate some spicy food, got heartburn, panicked, and came to the ER.

Castro has seen this exact presentation hundreds of times. He knows the playbook: Give her some antacids, maybe order an EKG to be safe, reassure her it's not a heart attack, send her home with a prescription for Prilosec and instructions to follow up with her primary care doctor.

Ten years ago, that's exactly what Castro would have done. The patient would have gone home. And she might have died.

Because here's the terrifying truth about emergency medicine: It's one of the highest-stakes environments in healthcare. Doctors have minutes to make life-or-death decisions with incomplete information. Diagnostic errors occur in about 5-7% of ER visits, and these errors contribute to an estimated 40,000-80,000 deaths annually in the U.S. alone.[50]

Castro knew these statistics cold. They haunted him. Because the thing about emergency medicine is that you're making decisions under the worst possible cognitive conditions: sleep deprivation, time pressure, emotional stress, cognitive overload from seeing 50+ patients per shift.

And even the best doctors - especially the best doctors - fall prey to cognitive biases. They anchor on the first diagnosis that comes to mind. They discount low-probability conditions. They miss atypical presentations of common diseases.

So when ChatGPT launched in late 2022, Castro didn't see a threat to his profession. He saw a potential solution to a problem that had plagued emergency medicine forever.

Phase 1: Castro Sets a Crystal-Clear Goal

Most doctors who started experimenting with ChatGPT had vague goals. "Be more efficient." "Save time on documentation." "Keep up with technology."

Castro's goal was different. And specific.

His goal: Use AI to reduce diagnostic errors by serving as a "second opinion" partner that could rapidly consider differential

---

50 Newman-Toker, David E., et al. "Serious Misdiagnosis-Related Harms in Malpractice Claims: The 'Big Three'—Vascular Events, Infections, and Cancers." *Diagnosis* 6, no. 3 (2019): 227-240, https://doi.org/10.1515/dx-2019-0019.

diagnoses he might miss under pressure - without replacing his clinical judgment or his relationship with patients.

Notice what Castro *didn't* say. He didn't say "use AI to diagnose patients" (that would be substitution). He didn't say "use AI to see more patients per hour" (that would be falling for the Productivity Paradox). He didn't say "use AI to handle the easy cases so I can focus on complex ones" (that could lead to skill atrophy).

His goal was laser-focused on the specific outcome that mattered most: **catching what he might miss when he was exhausted, rushed, and cognitively overwhelmed.**

This clarity was crucial. Because without a clear goal, you can't identify what actually drives results toward that goal. You end up throwing AI spaghetti at the wall and delivering no ROI.

Phase 2: Castro Identifies His 20%

With his goal defined, Castro did something most professionals never do: He ruthlessly distinguished between the many, many things he did every shift - and the small handful of things that actually drove his goal.

Was it spending more time on documentation? No. That consumed 40% of his shift but had zero impact on diagnostic accuracy.

Was it ordering more tests? No. That was easy to do but often unnecessary - and sometimes even harmful when it led to false positives and cascading interventions.

Castro's 20% that drove 80% of patient outcomes:

1. **Pattern recognition** - Quickly identifying which symptoms cluster into which conditions
2. **Differential diagnosis** - Considering the full range of possible causes, especially rare or atypical presentations
3. **Clinical reasoning** - Deciding which tests to order and how to interpret ambiguous results

Everything else was necessary but not sufficient. You can't be a great ER doctor without excellent bedside manner, without efficiency, without good documentation. But those things don't differentiate between a good outcome and a bad outcome in the moment when it matters most.

The problem? Under time pressure, fatigue, and cognitive load, even experienced physicians struggle with exactly these high-value activities. They anchor on the first diagnosis. They forget about rare conditions. They miss connections between symptoms.

But unlike most physicians, Castro didn't see these challenges as immovable boulders preventing better outcomes.

Instead, he saw an opportunity.

Phase 3: Castro Amplifies with AI

Here's what Castro developed - a systematic approach to using ChatGPT that amplified exactly the 20% that mattered most:

Step 1: He sees the patient, conducts the physical exam, takes the history, and forms his initial diagnostic impression -

just like always. AI doesn't replace this. AI can't replace this. You need human interaction to build rapport, pick up on subtle cues, and perform the physical examination.

Step 2: After forming his initial impression, he takes 90 seconds to input the case into ChatGPT on his phone. He's careful to remove all identifying information (HIPAA compliance matters). His prompt looks like this:

🙂 PROMPT

52-year-old female presents with chest pain. Describes burning sensation, worse after eating, radiating to throat. Vital signs: BP 142/88, HR 92, RR 16, O2 sat 98% on room air. Physical exam: mild epigastric tenderness, no chest wall tenderness, clear lungs, regular heart rhythm. No shortness of breath. Patient reports stress at work, hasn't been sleeping well. Generate a comprehensive differential diagnosis including both common and rare causes. Flag any critical 'can't miss' diagnoses. Suggest additional questions I should ask and tests that would help differentiate between possibilities.

Step 3: While waiting for the EKG results, he reviews ChatGPT's differential diagnosis. The AI generates a comprehensive list:

AI OUTPUT

> Common causes: GERD, peptic ulcer disease, costochondritis, anxiety
>
> Uncommon but serious causes: Acute coronary syndrome (atypical presentation), aortic dissection, pulmonary embolism, esophageal rupture
>
> Critical questions to ask: Any family history of heart disease or sudden cardiac death? Any recent long flights or leg swelling? Any history of connective tissue disorders?

And there it is. Buried in the list: **aortic dissection**.

Castro hadn't dismissed aortic dissection. He knew it was theoretically possible. But this patient looked stable. Her pain was clearly related to eating. She had obvious work stress. The diagnosis of GERD fit perfectly.

Under normal circumstances - well-rested, with plenty of time, on his 7th patient instead of his 47th - Castro would have caught this. He would have asked about family history. He would have been more thorough.

But at 3:47 AM, with a packed waiting room, running on four hours of sleep? The cognitive shortcut was already forming in his mind: *This is GERD, reassure and discharge.*

Step 4: Castro asks the additional questions ChatGPT suggested. Turns out the patient's father died suddenly of an aortic aneurysm at age 54. She also mentions that the pain started very suddenly about two hours ago - not gradually like typical heartburn.

Red flags everywhere. Castro immediately orders a CT angiogram.

The patient has an aortic dissection. She needs emergency surgery. If Castro had sent her home with antacids, she might have died—probably within 24 hours.

The critical point: ChatGPT didn't make the diagnosis. Castro did. ChatGPT didn't order the CT. Castro did. ChatGPT didn't save the patient's life. Castro did.

But ChatGPT expanded Castro's thinking at the exact moment when his human cognitive limitations were most dangerous. It compensated for his fatigue-induced tunnel vision. It reminded him to ask questions he might have skipped.

The result? Castro reports feeling more confident in his diagnostic accuracy while seeing the same number of patients. He's not working faster - he's working smarter. He's not seeing more patients - he's saving more lives.[51]

What Makes This Amplification Instead of Substitution?

Notice what Castro *doesn't* do:

---

51   Castro, Harvey. *ChatGPT Healthcare: Unlocking the Potential of Patient Empowerment and Clinical Excellence.* Independently published, 2023.

✘ He doesn't ask ChatGPT: "What is the diagnosis?" (That would be substitution - outsourcing his thinking)

✘ He doesn't accept ChatGPT's output uncritically (That would be dependency - letting his skills decay)

Instead, he leverages what AI is best at in concert with his unique expertise:

✔ AI generates a comprehensive list of diagnoses (leveraging its encyclopedic knowledge of every medical condition) → Castro applies clinical reasoning (leveraging his experience with thousands of actual patients)

✔ AI flags rare possibilities (compensating for human cognitive biases and fatigue) → Castro makes all final decisions (maintaining accountability, judgment, and the doctor-patient relationship)

This is the difference between the 95% who fail with AI and the 5% who soar.

And this is exactly the framework you're going to apply to your own micro-entrepreneurial project.

YOUR TURN: AMPLIFYING YOUR PROJECT WITH AI

Remember that project you started in Chapter 4? The one where you interviewed users, created compelling content, and led people to take action?

Now we're going to supercharge it using the Amplification Framework. Not by having AI do your work, but by using AI - in concert with your human skills - to do *better* work.

Over the three key phases, you're going to build out your project, step-by-step. By the end, you'll not only have completed your project, you'll have begun to develop the AI skills that will make you irreplaceable in your field.

Phase 1: Set Your Clear Goal

Castro's goal was "Reduce diagnostic errors by catching what I might miss under cognitive stress."

Notice what makes this powerful: It's about the specific *outcome* for his patients, not just an abstract, self-directed goal like "Use AI in my practice."

Your turn.

Step 1: Open your Surf Kit (available for free at THEJO-BINSIDERS.COM/SURF) and copy this prompt into your AI platform:

🗣️ **PROMPT**

I'm working on [describe your micro-entre-preneurial project from Chapter 4].

My target audience is [describe who you're serving].

Help me set a clear, measurable goal to deliver results for my audience.

Generate 3 goal options that are:

- Focused on tangible results
- Specific enough that I can measure success
- Achievable in the next few weeks

Step 2: Review the options and pick the goal that would create the most meaningful impact for your audience.

 **AI OUTPUT**

Excellent — you're thinking in terms of **impact**, not just activity. Here are three **clear, measurable goal options** for your Citizen's Guide to Environmental Data project, each achievable in three weeks and directly tied to audience outcomes.

🎯 **Goal Option 1: Measurable Behavior Change**

Goal:
Help **50 local residents** calculate their personal carbon footprints and commit to one specific reduction action within **3 weeks**.

How to Measure Success

- Number of residents who complete your footprint calculator or work-sheet (tracked via form, email signup, or QR code).
- Number of commitments recorded (e.g., "I'll bike to work twice a week").

> **Why It Works**
> You'll directly observe how your guide leads
> people from **awareness** → **engagement** → **behav-**
> **ior change** — a core EdTech-style learning
> funnel.

*Every great project has a North Star. Make sure that
you're excited about yours before you dive in!*

Here are some examples based on the scenarios from Chapter 4.

Data Analyst's Sustainability Guide

✖ **Bad goal (Substitution):** "Use AI to analyze environmental data faster"

✔ **Good goal (Amplification):** "Help 10 community members take one concrete action to reduce their carbon footprint based on local climate data"

EdTech Marketer's YouTube Channel

✖ **Bad goal (Substitution):** "Use AI to instantly research my market"

✔ **Good goal (Amplification):** "Identify the 3 biggest pain points teachers face with classroom technology across a diverse series of interviews"

Mechanical Engineer's Leadership Substack

✖ **Bad goal (Substitution):** "Use AI to solve leadership challenges"

✔ **Good goal** (**Amplification**): "Research and write about engineering leadership deeply enough that 25 peers sign up for my newsletter"

See the difference? Substitution goals are about using AI to do your existing work faster. Amplification goals are about creating specific outcomes for your audience - outcomes that would matter even if AI didn't exist.

Write your goal down. That's your North Star for the rest of the project.

Phase 2: Identify Your Pareto Driver

Castro identified that differential diagnosis - considering the full range of possible conditions under time pressure - drove 80% of his diagnostic accuracy.

Now you're going to identify the single most important driver for your project.

Step 1: Copy this prompt into your AI platform:

🤔 PROMPT

Here's my project and goal: [describe from the previous section]

Break my project down into a series of tasks and suggest which three tasks are most Pareto important to achieve my goal.

Step 2: You now have an 80/20 project plan that you can use in the final stage to really focus your efforts when it comes time to execute.

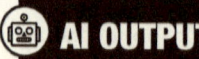 **AI OUTPUT**

The 3 Most Pareto-Important Tasks

1. Recruiting and enrolling participants (Task 6)
Without enough participants, nothing else happens.

Focus: Simple signup + clear "why it matters" message.

2. Helping participants calculate their footprints (Task 10)
This is the core activity — the moment of awareness.

Make it **easy and guided** so no one drops off due to confusion.

3. Ensuring each person commits to one concrete action (Task 13)
This is your impact metric.

Provide **5-10 easy, locally relevant choices** and make the commitment public (or logged).

One of the best things about AI is that it's not afraid of calling out sacred cows - e.g., busywork or stalling tactics. Let it be your Project Coach to keep your eyes on the prize!

Here are some examples of top Pareto Drivers for different projects:

Data Analyst's Sustainability Guide

✔ **Pareto Driver:** Making it so easy to understand the climate data that people can't help but take a concrete action

Why it's essential: This is what actually changes behavior. AI can gather data and create charts, but only humans can figure out which levers will motivate their specific community to take action. This requires synthesizing climate science + local context + behavioral psychology.

✘ **Not Pareto:** Gathering raw climate data (AI can do this quickly; doesn't require a human's unique judgment about a specific audience)

EdTech Marketer's YouTube Channel

✔ **Pareto Driver:** Asking the follow-up questions during interviews that reveal the real pain point hiding beneath the surface complaint

Why it's essential: Teachers start by describing surface problems ("Our WiFi is slow"), but the real pain is deeper ("I'm not actually moving the needle on learning because I'm spending most of my time doing tech support"). AI can transcribe interviews, but only a human can hear the shift in a teacher's voice and ask "Tell me more about that" at exactly the right moment. That human intuition is what makes other teachers say "Finally, someone gets it!"

✘ **Not Pareto:** Transcribing video footage (AI can handle transcribing easily; doesn't require any human judgment about what makes an interview powerful)

Mechanical Engineer's Leadership Substack

✔ **Pareto Driver:** Synthesizing leadership research with real engineering team dynamics to identify which practices actually work in technical environments (versus which sound good but fail)

Why it's essential: Generic leadership advice is everywhere. Engineering managers need someone who can say "Here's what the research says - and here's why it fails with junior engineers, plus what to do instead." AI can summarize research, but only humans can filter it through years of leading actual engineering teams, knowing which advice translates and which doesn't.

✘ **Not Pareto:** Formatting articles for Substack (AI can handle layout and formatting; doesn't require a human's hard-won team leadership experience)

Phase 3: Amplify with AI

Castro used AI to generate comprehensive differential diagnoses while he maintained clinical reasoning. You're going to use AI to amplify your Pareto Drivers while maintaining the judgment that creates real impact.

Step 1: Copy this prompt into your AI platform:

PROMPT

Here's my project and goal: [describe from the previous section]

Build out a full project plan around the 3 most Pareto important tasks to achieve this goal and, for each one, delegate the specific steps to either AI or me based on our comparative advantages.

For everything that you delegate to AI, suggest a sample prompt or tool I can use to execute that step.

Step 2: Start to execute your project plan, leveraging both your own expertise and AI's strengths.

AI OUTPUT

⚡ PARETO TASK 1: Recruit and Enroll Participants

◎ **Objective:** Sign up **50 residents** by the end of **Week 1** using a mix of AI-powered outreach and authentic personal engagement.

☑ **Deliverable:** A confirmed list of **50 participants** with contact info.

STEP	DESCRIPTION	DELEGATE TO	WHY	AI PROMPT OR TOOL
1. **Identify your audience**	Choose your community segment (neighbor-hood, school, club).	You	You know the social dynamics and best channels.	—
2. **Write engaging outreach messages**	Draft emails, flyers, and social media posts that invite participation.	AI	AI can generate multiple tone/ style variations quickly.	**Prompt:** "Write 3 friendly outreach posts inviting local residents to join a 3-week '50 Residents, 1 Action' challenge to calculate their carbon footprint and commit to one small change. Tone: warm, local, hopeful."

One of the best AI use cases is breaking a complicated project down into doable tasks. The next time you feel like procrastinating, don't be afraid to ask AI to crush that giant boulder into more manageable chunks.

Here's what that AI-human hybrid work looks like across our three examples:

Data Analyst's Sustainability Guide

What AI handled:

- Processed 50 climate studies (would have taken days of manual reading)
- Generated dozens of visualization options (hours of design work)
- Created tracking infrastructure for commitments (eliminated spreadsheet setup)

What the analyst did:

- Read top studies deeply to understand nuance (requires critical thinking AI can't replicate)
- Selected 3 actions matching the specific community's values (requires local knowledge)
- Rewrote explanations in locally meaningful language (requires understanding what resonates with neighbors)
- Personally followed up with community members (requires human relationship and accountability)

The result: A guide that drives actual behavior change because it combines AI's analytical horsepower with the analyst's deep community knowledge. AI made it possible to process vast amounts of data; the analyst made it relevant enough that people actually took action.

EdTech Marketer's YouTube Channel

What AI handled:

- Transcribed hours of interviews with timestamps (eliminated days of typing)
- Handled technical video editing - cutting, audio, b-roll (saved hours of production work)
- Optimized titles, descriptions, thumbnails (faster than learning YouTube SEO)

What the marketer did:

- Earned trust to get teachers to commit to being interviewed (requires showing up as real person)
- Asked follow-up questions revealing real pain (requires reading emotion in the moment)
- Identified which 3 pain points were most critical (requires judgment about what connects and resonates)
- Crafted narrative arc honoring what teachers meant (requires deep audience understanding)

The result: A series of videos that reveal the root cause of educational challenges because they combine AI's production efficiency with the marketer's human intuition. AI made it possible to produce polished video quickly; the marketer made it powerful enough that teachers felt truly understood.

Engineer's Leadership Substack

What AI handled:

- Researched 30 leadership articles and synthesized recommendations (hours of reading compressed to minutes)
- Created initial outlines (eliminated blank page problem)
- Formatted for Substack with proper citations (handled technical publishing details)

What the engineer did:

- Filtered recommendations through real team experience (requires pattern recognition from hundreds of situations)
- Brought the outline to life through their own unique voice (requires having a clear viewpoint and style)
- Replaced generic examples with real team stories (requires vulnerability and honesty)
- Added critical nuance about when practices fail (requires having seen things go wrong)

The result: A newsletter that gets 25+ managers to subscribe because it combines AI's research speed with the engineer's hard-won wisdom about what really works. AI made it possible to survey the landscape quickly; the engineer made it trustworthy enough that busy managers actually read and leveraged the recommendations.

WHY THIS PROJECT MATTERS

At this point, you may be thinking: "Great - I did all that work just to get 10 people to take action!"

But what's way more important than *what* you did is *how* you did it.

Because the future is super clear in one regard: We'll all be working with AI for the rest of our careers.

And we can spend that time competing against AI - or succeeding **with** it.

Which means that this meta-skill - of learning how to use AI in concert with our human strengths - is almost certain to become the defining skill of our times.

Because just like Dr. Harvey Castro's human-and-AI-powered heroics at 3:47 AM, it's the professionals who master the full power of that combination who will truly own the future.

THE FELLOWSHIP FACTOR

But here's the thing about developing AI skills: You can't do it in isolation.

As you saw in all of the project examples, AI intuition comes from building real things for real people. Because the ultimate AI accelerant isn't taking a prompt engineering class - it's having a community of people who are counting on you to take your game to the next level.

In other words, you need fellowship.

And fellowship - real human connection in a world of AI fakery - isn't just nice to have. It's the ultimate competitive advantage. Read on to learn why...

6

FINISH WITH FELLOWSHIP

t's August 2008, and Brian Chesky is drowning.

He's 25 years old, living in San Francisco, and he can't make rent. His credit cards are maxed out. He's been pitching his startup idea - renting air mattresses in people's apartments - to investors for months, and the responses have been universally dismissive.

"Air mattresses? In strangers' homes? That's the dumbest idea I've ever heard."

Chesky has exactly $1,000 in the bank. His co-founder Joe Gebbia is in the same boat. They need to either quit their dream or find a way to survive long enough to prove everyone wrong.

Then Chesky remembers something his industrial design professor told him years ago: "Your network isn't who you know. It's who knows *what you can do.*"

So Chesky makes a phone call to Michael Seibel, a fellow startup founder he'd met at the South by Southwest conference earlier that year. They'd grabbed coffee, exchanged a few emails, and stayed in touch in spite of their hectic lives.

Chesky's pitch is brutally honest: "We're building this company. We're broke. We need help. Would you look at what we're doing?"

Seibel agrees to meet. After 30 minutes of hearing Chesky's vision, he makes a single introduction: Paul Graham, founder of Y Combinator, the most prestigious startup accelerator in the world.

That introduction led to Y Combinator accepting Airbnb into their program. Y Combinator provided $20,000 in funding, mentorship, and - most importantly - credibility. That credibility helped Airbnb raise their first real funding round. That funding helped them build the platform. That platform became a $75 billion company.[52]

Here's the part that matters: Chesky's product hadn't changed. His skills hadn't changed. His business plan was the same one that every investor had rejected.

What changed? **He activated a relationship.**

Not a business card. Not a LinkedIn contact. But a genuine human relationship activated when it mattered most.

This is Fellowship - the 'F' in SURF. And here's why it matters more than ever: In an age when AI can already do so much and is growing smarter with each new generation, **our relationships are our truly *sustainable* competitive advantage.**

---

52 "The Airbnb Story: How Three Ordinary Guys Disrupted an Industry," *Leigh Gallagher*, Houghton Mifflin Harcourt, 2017.

INTRODUCING THE HUMAN ALGORITHM

To understand why relationships are so essential to our long-term success, let's consider how they factor into one of the key moments of every career: Hiring.

We'll start with the most important hiring stat of all:

Referred candidates are 20X more likely to be hired than online applicants.[53]

And I know what you're thinking: "No duh, Jeremy - referred candidates *always* do better." But now read the stat again and, this time, focus not on the *what* but the *why.*

Specifically, why are referred candidates not just treated a little better, but *massively* better? Do recruiters just love their own referral processes? Or loathe online applicants?

It turns out that the answer isn't bias. It's biology.

Because the most important algorithm of all isn't the one that's powering ChatGPT, but the one that's running between all of our ears: **The Human Algorithm.**

Your Caveman Brain Is Running Your Career (And Everyone Else's)

To understand how the Human Algorithm works, let's think about what's actually happening in every recruiter's brain when they review your application.

---

53 Gem. *2025 Recruiting Benchmarks*. San Francisco, CA: Gem, 2025. https://lp.gem.com/rs/972-IVV-330/images/2025%20Recruiting%20Benchmarks%20-%20Gem.pdf.

First of all, recognize that our brains have a fundamental trust hierarchy that was burned into our neural circuitry over 300,000 years of human evolution:[54]

- **Members of our tribe = Good.**
- **Strangers = Dangerous.**

This hierarchy exists for a simple reason: On the African savanna, trusting the wrong person meant death. Your ancestors who were too trusting of strangers got killed. Your ancestors who carefully vetted unknown people survived and passed on their genes.

Which means every human alive today - including your recruiter - is descended from the paranoid ones.

But how did a fundamentally wary species ultimately work together enough to build cities, civilization, and ChatGPT?

Research by evolutionary anthropologist Robin Dunbar reveals that humans can only maintain direct social relationships with about 150 people - a number limited by our brain's processing capacity.[55] So in order to grow past this cap, we needed to add a new level to our trust hierarchy:

- **Friends of our tribe = Most likely good.**

54   Dunbar, Robin I. M. "The Social Brain Hypothesis and Its Implications for Social Evolution." *Annals of Human Biology* 36, no. 5 (2009): 562-572.

55   Dunbar, Robin. "The Anatomy of Friendship." *Trends in Cognitive Sciences* 22, no. 1 (2018): 32-51.

That cooperation-by-association is how tribes became villages, villages became city-states, and city-states became nations.

And that phenomenon is still playing out every time you apply for a job:

When you apply online, you're a stranger. A potential threat. Someone who needs to be carefully evaluated and probably rejected.

But when you're referred, you just went from Stranger to Friend of the Tribe. Which means your recruiter's brain doesn't trigger the same threat response. In fact, research from neuroeconomist Paul Zak shows that when people receive information from trusted sources, their brains release oxytocin - a neurochemical that promotes trust and social bonding.[56]

This creates what Zak calls "virtuous cycles" where trust breeds more trust. The recruiter trusts their colleague. Their colleague vouches for you. Therefore, the recruiter's brain automatically extends provisional trust to you - before they've even read your resume.

That's why referred candidates aren't just slightly favored. They're operating in a completely different neural category.

And that's why the Human Algorithm matters even more than the AI one.

---

56 Zak, Paul J. "The Neuroscience of Trust." *Harvard Business Review*, January-February 2017, https://hbr.org/2017/01/the-neuroscience-of-trust.

The AI Trust Collapse:
Why Relationships Matter
More Than Ever

But here's where things get really interesting - and where your relational advantage becomes even more pronounced.

The trust gap between strangers and known connections has always existed. But in 2025, it's becoming a canyon.

Why? Because AI has made it impossible to trust what you see from strangers.

Consider what recruiters face today:

- **AI-generated resumes** that perfectly match job descriptions but may not reflect real skills
- **Fake LinkedIn profiles** with AI-generated photos and accomplishments
- **AI-enhanced video interviews** where candidates use AI cheating tools on their screens to generate scripted answers

It's gotten so bad that the majority of recruiters - 60% - have now caught an applicant misrepresenting themselves.[57] And even the big tech companies that pioneered video calls (e.g., Google, Cisco) are now going back to in-person interviews to weed out the AI fakers.[58]

---

57 Williams, Wayne. "Employers Admit Candidates Faking Identities with AI Are Outsmarting Them, with Fraudulent Hires Costing Companies Thousands." *TechRadar Pro*, September 30, 2025. https://www.techradar.com/pro/employers-admit-candidates-faking-identities-with-ai-are-outsmarting-them-with-fraudulent-hires-costing-companies-thousands

58 Smith, Ray A. "AI Is Forcing the Return of the In-Person Job Interview." *Wall Street Journal*, August 12, 2025. https://www.wsj.com/lifestyle/careers/ai-job-interview-virtual-in-person-305f9fd0

Think about what this means: Every signal that recruiters used to rely on when evaluating strangers has been compromised. Your resume? Could be AI-generated. Your portfolio? Might be fake. Your interview answers? Possibly coached by AI in real-time.

Except one signal remains uncompromised: **The word of someone they already trust.**

When your former colleague says "I worked with Sarah for three years and she's phenomenal," that's not something AI can fake. That's a real human, with a real reputation they're putting on the line, making a real attestation about your real abilities.

And recruiters are clinging to that last real signal like a life raft. Just look at the data (see Figure 6.1):

- **2016:** 6% of referred candidates get hired vs. .7% of online applicants[59]
- **2025:** 10% of referred candidates get hired vs. .5% of online applicants[60]

In less than 10 years, referrals went from conferring a 9X advantage over online applicants to a 20X advantage.

59   Lever, Inc. *The Little Grey Book of Recruiting Benchmarks 2016*. San Francisco: Lever, 2016. PDF file. https://myejst.org/wp-content/uploads/2017/04/the-little-grey-book-of-recruiting-benchmarks-2016.pdf.

60   Gem. *2025 Recruiting Benchmarks*. San Francisco, CA: Gem, 2025. https://lp.gem.com/rs/972-IVV-330/images/2025%20Recruiting%20Benchmarks%20-%20Gem.pdf.

Figure 6.1 - Hiring Rates: Referrals vs. Online Applications

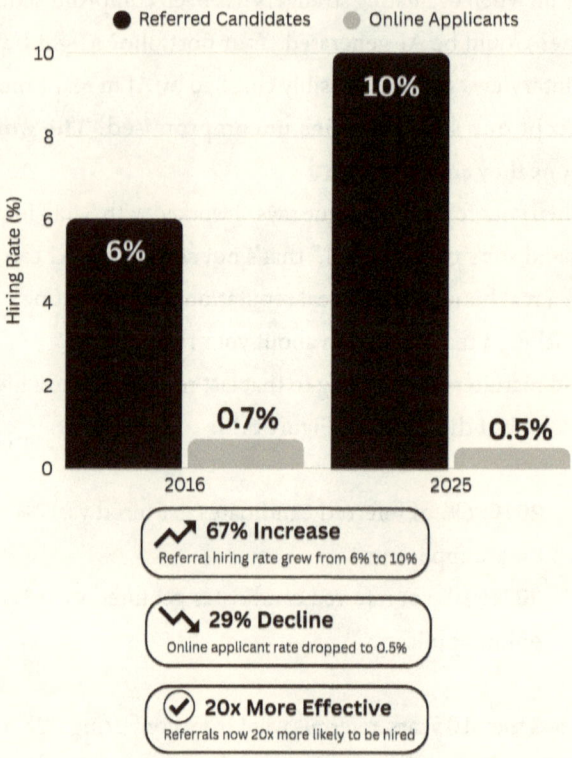

This was one of the most shocking stats I uncovered while writing this book. AI isn't just making human relationships a little more important - it's absolutely turbocharging them!

Which means the question is no longer "Should I build relationships?"

The question is now: "Can I afford not to?"

WHY "TRADITIONAL" NETWORKING IS DEEPLY UNTRADITIONAL

(And What to Do Instead)

"But I hate networking," you're thinking. "All those awkward conferences, forced small talk, collecting business cards from people I'll never see again, pretending to care about someone's job when I'm really just waiting to pitch mine..."

Good. You should hate that. Because traditional networking is actually totally... **untraditional**.

Think about what actually happens at a typical networking event:

- A stranger approaches you at a conference
- You exchange pleasantries about the buffet lunch
- The stranger asks you what you do
- When your answer doesn't match what he's looking for, he feigns an excuse to step away and says "Let's connect on LinkedIn!"
- You never speak again

Does any of that sound like the kinds of deep trust-building that helped us survive back on the savanna?

Nope. In fact, those are the exact behaviors that made us suspicious of strangers in the first place.

Which is why studies show that people can detect self-interested motivations with 90% accuracy, even in brief interactions.[61]

---

61 DePaulo, Bella M., et al. "Lying in Everyday Life." *Journal of Personality and Social Psychology* 70, no. 5 (1996): 979-995.

And what does The Human Algorithm do when it detects this transactional behavior that our ancient ancestors evolved to avoid? It shuts down. Puts up walls. Files you under "Person who can't be trusted."

The 3 Types of Professional Relationships

But it turns out there's a better way to connect that honors the relationships our species has trusted for millennia.

To identify this approach, Wharton professor Adam Grant studied networking patterns across thousands of professionals and identified three fundamental relational styles:[62]

- **Takers** (strive to get more than they give)
- **Matchers** (aim for equal exchanges - quid pro quo)
- **Givers** (contribute to others without expecting immediate return)

Grant's research revealed something counterintuitive: While Givers can sometimes end up at the bottom of success metrics (when they give too much without boundaries), they also dominate the top. The most successful professionals across industries tend to be strategic Givers - people who help others generously but also maintain focus on their own goals.[63]

---

62 Grant, Adam. *Give and Take: Why Helping Others Drives Our Success*. New York: Penguin Books, 2013.

63 Ibid.

Here's the breakdown from Grant's research:

- **Bottom performers:** Selfless Givers (burned out from helping everyone)
- **Middle performers:** Takers and Matchers (transactional relationships)
- **Top performers:** Strategic Givers (generous but with boundaries)

The traditional "work the room" networking strategy? That's Taker behavior wearing a Matcher costume. You're essentially saying: "I'm investing time in you now because I want something from you later."

And our Human Algorithm can tell.

What Actually Works: Strategic Giving

So here's the networking strategy that actually matches our neural wiring:

Don't network to get. Network to give.

Strategic giving means:

- **Helping people without a specific ask in mind** (although not helping everyone indiscriminately)
- **Making valuable introductions between people** (connecting your network to each other)

- **Sharing knowledge and expertise freely** (teaching what you know)
- **Following up with genuine interest** (not just when you need something)

Stanford professor Frank Flynn studied this approach and found that strategic Givers have the highest professional status in organizations - outdoing both Takers and Matchers.[64] Why? Because when you help people without immediate expectation of return, The Human Algorithm categorizes you much more as a fellow "tribe member" than "potential threat."

And here's the beautiful part: You don't need to be an extrovert to do this. You don't need to "work the room" at conferences. You don't need to collect hundreds of business cards.

You need to build real relationships with a small number of people who matter.

Grant's research found that successful Givers typically maintain deep relationships with 10-15 key people in their field, plus looser connections with maybe 50-100 others.[65] Not thousands. Not even hundreds of deep relationships.

Just a small core of people who actually know you, trust you, and would vouch for you.

---

64   Flynn, Francis J. "How Much Should I Give and How Often? The Effects of Generosity and Frequency of Favor Exchange on Social Status and Productivity." *Academy of Management Journal* 46, no. 5 (2003): 539-553.

65   Grant, Adam. *Give and Take: Why Helping Others Drives Our Success.* New York: Penguin Books, 2013.

Your Gift: The Generativity Secret

But here's the question everyone asks: "If I'm looking to start or change a career, what can I possibly give someone who's *already* successful?"

The answer lies in one of the most powerful - and misunderstood - psychological drives in human nature.

Because while it's true that you're unlikely to give an existing expert the gift of even deeper expertise, there is one gift that every expert craves: **Generativity.**

This phenomenon was identified by psychologist Erik Erikson as a fundamental human drive that typically emerges in middle adulthood: the desire to guide and nurture the next generation.[66]

Think about it: When was the last time someone asked you about your career journey, your biggest lessons, what you wish you'd known earlier? How did it make you feel?

Most people light up. Because generativity isn't altruism - it's a biological need.

Neuroscientist Emily Falk and her colleagues used fMRI brain scans to discover what happens when people share information they find valuable. They found significant activation in brain regions associated with reward processing - including areas that respond to food and money.[67]

---

66 Erikson, Erik H. *Identity and the Life Cycle*. New York: W. W. Norton & Company, 1980.

67 Falk, Emily B., et al. "Creating Buzz: The Neural Correlates of Effective Message Propagation." *Psychological Science* 24, no. 7 (2013): 1234-1242.

In other words, sharing knowledge literally activates our brain's reward system. When you ask someone for their wisdom, you're not taking from them - you're giving them a neurological reward.

That's the gift of generativity. And this is why strategic giving works so powerfully:

Asking an expert for wisdom (not favors) → Activates their generativity drive → Creates intrinsic motivation to help

Research from Harvard Business School proves this dynamic. Alison Wood Brooks and her colleagues found that people who ask for advice are perceived as more competent than those who don't ask at all. The researchers concluded that "seeking advice is a surprisingly effective strategy for exercising influence when we lack authority."[68]

Why? Because asking thoughtful questions signals two things simultaneously:

1. You value their expertise (activates their generativity)
2. You're committed to growth (makes them want to invest in your success)

But here's the critical caveat: This only works if you're genuinely trying to learn, not just using them for your own purposes.

As mentioned before, research shows that people can detect insincerity with remarkable accuracy, even in brief interactions.[69]

---

68   Brooks, Alison Wood, et al. "Smart People Ask for (My) Advice: Seeking Advice Boosts Perceptions of Competence." *Management Science* 61, no. 6 (2015): 1421-1435.

69   DePaulo, Bella M., et al. "Lying in Everyday Life." *Journal of Personality and Social Psychology* 70, no. 5 (1996): 979-995.

Our brains are finely tuned to spot when someone is faking interest versus genuinely curious.

The Human Algorithm can tell the difference between:

- **Transactional:** "I'm really interested in your experience at Google - can you tell me how to get a job there?" (triggers suspicion)
- **Generative:** "I'm totally intrigued by your tech journey - what advice would you give someone who wants to follow in your footsteps?" (triggers generosity)

So the strategy isn't "fake interest in people to shake them down." It's "become genuinely curious about how people built their careers, because their wisdom will help you build yours."

And when you later need their help - when you're job searching or making a career transition - they'll remember you as the person who valued their experience. Not the person who set off their Human Algorithm alarm bells.

That's the difference between networking that feels gross and relationship-building that's as natural as our very DNA.

The New Networking Equation

Here's what all this means about how to approach networking in the Age of AI:

Old networking: Meet 100 people in the hopes that you find someone who can help you achieve *your* goals → Turn off 99 of those people in the process → Waste tons of time while also burning bridges

New networking: Build deep relationships with 10 people by seeking *their* advice → Engage their generative impulses → Create sustainable relationships that are fruitful for both parties for years to come

This isn't about being introverted or extroverted. It's about being strategic.

Just like Brian Chesky realized he couldn't bring Airbnb to life totally on his own, strategic networking is about identifying people you can learn from and being humble enough to seek their expertise.

So the question going forward *isn't* "How do I force myself to enjoy networking events?"

Instead, it's: "How do I build a small number of deep relationships that actually matter?"

And that's exactly what we're going to do in the rest of this chapter.

THE FELLOWSHIP FRAMEWORK: 3 STEPS TO BUILDING RELATIONSHIPS THAT MATTER

Alright, enough theory. Let's get tactical.

Remember in Chapter 3 when you identified your ikigai and reached out to people doing the work you want to do? You had conversations with professionals in your target field, learned about their journeys, and got valuable insights about the role.

Those weren't just informational interviews. Those were the first steps toward **building your tribe.**

Now we're going to systematically deepen those relationships using everything we've learned about The Human Algorithm, strategic giving, and generativity.

Here's your three-step framework:

- **Step 1:** Reconnect with Your Tribe
- **Step 2:** Deepen Through Generative Learning
- **Step 3:** Sustain with Strategic Giving

This framework works because it honors how The Human Algorithm actually operates: You're not approaching strangers. You're reconnecting with people who already know you - and leveraging the power of referrals to expand your network further.

Let's break down each step.

Step 1: Reconnect with Your Tribe

Your Chapter 3 conversations may have seemed focused on a very limited purpose: helping you validate your career direction.

But here's what you may not have realized: **Those people are now part of your tribe.** Not in the shallow LinkedIn sense - in the real, Human Algorithmic sense. Because unlike someone you randomly connect with online, you actually had the guts to strike up a conversation in the real world.

Which means reconnecting isn't starting from zero. It's building on established trust. And so now it's time to take that trust to the next level by reconnecting.

Here's a sample template to get you started:

 Subject: Update on [what you discussed in Chapter 3]

Hi [name],

I hope you're doing well! We spoke a few months ago when I was exploring [target field/role], and your insights about [specific thing they said] really stuck with me.

Since then, I actually built [brief description of your project from Chapters 4-5] based on your advice to [specific advice they shared].

I'd love to get your perspective on where I should focus next. Specifically, I'm trying to figure out [1-2 specific questions about skills to develop or next steps].

Would you have 15 minutes in the next few weeks for a quick call? I'd really value your guidance.

Thanks for considering,

[your name]

P.S. Here's a link to the project if you're curious: [link]

Notice what this reconnection does:

✔ **Honors their previous contribution** ("your insights really stuck with me")

✔ **Proves you took action** (you built something real)

✔ **Shows you're not a Taker** (you didn't just come back when you need a job)

✔ **Activates generativity** (asking for guidance on growth, not favors)

✔ **Provides proof of seriousness** (link to your actual work)

In other words, catnip for our Human Algorithm!

So set a goal to reconnect with 3 people from your Chapter 3 conversations this week.

And based on the trust you've already established, expect 60-80% to respond positively. Why? Because by walking the talk on that initial conversation, you've just moved from Stranger to Member of the Tribe.

Step 2: Deepen Through Generative Learning

When someone agrees to reconnect, keep in mind that this conversation has a different purpose than your Chapter 3 call.

In Chapter 3, you were testing: *"Is this the right path for me?"*

Now you're deepening to: *"How do I succeed on this path?"*

So here are the three questions that matter most:

Question 1: *"How did you get to where you are? What were the pivotal moments or decisions that really mattered?"*

This is the generativity jackpot. You're asking someone to reflect on their entire career journey and identify the moments that defined them.

Research shows that people derive tremendous satisfaction from having their life story witnessed and valued by others.[70] When you ask this question, you're essentially saying: "Your journey matters. I want to learn from it."

And notice what you're NOT asking: "How do I get your job?" or "What's the fastest path to success?" Those questions make it about you extracting value. This question makes it about honoring their experience.

The answers you get will be gold. Because unlike generic career advice, you'll hear the real story: the lucky breaks, the hard choices, the pivots they didn't see coming. And those stories contain wisdom that no blog post or LinkedIn article can capture.

Question 2: *"Where do you see this space heading in the next few years - and what types of people will be best positioned?"*

Now that they've shared their past, this question invites them to think about the future - specifically, YOUR future.

---

70 Adler, Jonathan M., and Dan P. McAdams. "Telling Stories About Therapy: Ego Development, Narrative Coherence, and Well-Being." Journal of Personality 75, no. 6 (2007): 1171–1196. https://doi.org/10.1111/j.1467-6494.2007.00471.x.

This works because it activates their expertise in a forward-looking way. They're not just recounting history; they're using their pattern recognition to predict what's coming next. And by asking about "types of people" rather than "skills," you're getting them to think holistically - about mindset, relationships, positioning - not just technical abilities.

Here's the brilliant part: When they describe the types of people who'll succeed, they're subconsciously creating a template for you to follow. You're not asking "Will I succeed?" (puts them on the spot). You're asking them to paint a picture of success, which you can then map yourself onto.

Question 3: *"If you were in my shoes right now - with my experience and trying to [describe your goal] - what's the ONE thing you would focus on?"*

This is where everything converges. They've told you their story. They've shared their vision of the future. Now you're asking them to synthesize all of that wisdom into a single piece of actionable advice—specifically for you.

The power of this question comes from three things:

1. **The perspective-taking** ("if you were in my shoes") activates their empathy and makes them mentally inhabit your situation
2. **The specificity** (referencing your actual goal) prevents generic platitudes
3. **The word "ONE"** forces prioritization - they can't give you a laundry list; they have to tell you what matters MOST

Research shows this type of perspective-taking creates the strongest mentorship bonds.[71] When someone imagines themselves in your position and gives you their best advice, they become psychologically invested in your success. They've put themselves on the line. They want to see if their guidance works.

And here's what usually happens: Three months later, when you send them a progress update showing you took their advice (we'll cover this in Step 3), they'll feel that neurological reward we talked about earlier. You've proven their wisdom mattered. You've closed the generativity loop.

Question 4: *"This has been so awesome - you've given me a real sense of direction that I didn't have coming into this chat. To keep that momentum going, is there one person you admire in this space who you'd recommend I connect with?"*

Here's where strategic fellowship becomes exponential.

Because the powerful thing about relationships is that one trusted bond often leads directly to the next one - especially if you nudge it along.

And so by asking for a specific recommendation, you're taking the trust you've built up with the initial contact and transferring it to the next contact like so:

---

71 Bonaccio, S., & Dalal, R. S. (2006). "Advice taking and decision-making: An integrative literature review, and implications for the organizational sciences." *Organizational Behavior and Human Decision Processes*, 101(2), 127-151. https://doi.org/10.1016/j.obhdp.2006.07.001

Subject: [Original Contact] suggested I reach out

Hi [New Person],

I recently spoke with [Original Contact] about [topic/field], and when I asked who else I should learn from, your name came up immediately.

I'm exploring [your target field/goal] and recently built [one-sentence project description]. I'd love to get your perspective on [specific question related to their expertise].

Would you have 15 minutes for a quick call in the next few weeks?

Thanks for considering!

[your name]

P.S. Here's my project if you're curious: [link]

And remember: Each person you meet through this method is starting at a "friend of the tribe" trust level - not "stranger." Which means they're exponentially more likely to take your call, give you real advice, and potentially introduce you to others in THEIR network.

This is how small networks become powerful ones. Not through collecting hundreds of LinkedIn connections, but through systematically building trust-based relationships that compound over time.

Step 3: Sustain with Strategic Giving

Here's where most people completely drop the ball. They have a great conversation, learn all these critical insights, and then... nothing. Radio silence until they need something.

Big mistake.

Because remember what we learned about the evolution of the Human Algorithm: Originally, trust only extended to members of your tribe - i.e., the people you saw and interacted with every single day at a time when your entire world was the 150 or fewer people who lived around you. And so it was easy to maintain trust with the tribe because you were getting pro-social signals on a daily basis.

But in order to extend that trust to Friends of the Tribe, we also had to find a way to keep renewing that trust. And that's where the "check-in" came from. What might have started with a seasonal hunting visit to a neighboring tribe has now blossomed into annual holiday cards, quarterly catch-up lunches, and even the occasional FaceTime that harkens back to the original face time!

As with most things in life, it turns out that the key here is quality vs. quantity. Research from Stanford shows that relationships remain active with just **4 meaningful touches per year.**[72] That's once per quarter. Not weekly. Not even monthly.

But those touches need to be *meaningful* - which means they need to demonstrate strategic giving, not just "staying top of mind."

So let's start with an easy example - the message you should be sending within 24 hours of every important conversation:

---

72   Dunbar, R. I. M. (2018). "The Anatomy of Friendship." *Trends in Cognitive Sciences*, 22(1), 32-51. https://doi.org/10.1016/j.tics.2017.10.004

Hi [name],

Thank you so much for the conversation yesterday. Your insight about [specific thing they said] completely changed how I'm thinking about [specific challenge].

I'm now planning to [specific action based on their advice]. I'll let you know how it goes!

Thanks again for your generosity with both your time and wisdom. I can't wait to build upon everything you've shared with me.

[your name]

This follow-up does three things:

1. **Proves you listened** (references specific insights)
2. **Shows their advice mattered** (you're taking action)
3. **Emphasizes generativity** (connects their wisdom to the next generation)

This is strategic giving reinforced: You're not just taking their wisdom, you're demonstrating its impact *and* giving back.

Now here's how you stay in touch without overwhelming yourself or them.

- Sign-up for a dead-simple and free tool called Follow-UpThen (FOLLOWUPTHEN.COM)
- Add the following address to the Bcc line of your message: EVERY3MONTHS@FOLLOWUPTHEN.COM
- Just like clockwork, you'll get reminded on a quarterly basis to make one of the four types of meaningful touchpoints

Touchpoint 1: The Progress Update

Hi [name],

Quick update: Remember when you suggested I [their advice]? I tried it and [specific result]. Your guidance was spot-on.

[Optional: One sentence on current project status]

Thanks again for taking time to share your expertise. It made a real difference.

This is the most powerful touch because it closes the generativity loop. They gave you wisdom, you acted on it, and now you're showing them the impact. That neurological reward we discussed earlier? You just delivered it.

Touchpoint 2: The Valuable Share

> Hi [name],
>
> I came across [article/tool/opportunity] and immediately thought of you based on our conversation about [topic]. [One sentence on why it's relevant.]
>
> Hope you find it useful!

This reinforces that you're a strategic giver, not a taker. You're adding value to their life, not just extracting from it.

Touchpoint 3: The Genuine Congratulation

> Hi [name],
>
> Just saw your [promotion/article/project] on LinkedIn. Congratulations! Given what you told me about [something from your conversation], this must be especially gratifying.

This shows you're paying attention to their career, not just using them for yours.

Touchpoint 4: The Introduction

```
Hi [Person A] and [Person B],

I wanted to introduce you two because [specific
reason based on your conversations with each].

[Person A], [Person B] has expertise in [area]
and recently [relevant accomplishment].

[Person B], [Person A] is working on [project/
challenge] that relates to [Person B's inter-
est].

I thought you'd both benefit from connecting!
```

This last touchpoint is especially important because it sets the stage for you to go from a mere novice in your field to a connector. Just like your initial contacts laid the groundwork for your future success, you're already pivoting into that generative role yourself!

The Compound Effect of Fellowship

Although these steps may feel like a lot of work to build a relatively small number of relationships, remember that relationships are compounding - both in terms of numbers and depth.

Here's what happens when you consistently apply this framework:

Month 1: You reconnect with existing contacts and have deeper conversations because you've already earned their trust.

Month 2: You build new connections based on the recommendations of your existing contacts.

Month 3: You follow-up with your original contacts which marks you as a rare breed - the kind of person who actually bothers to stay in touch.

Months 4-6: Your new connections recommend even newer connections - while at the same time trusting you more based on your follow-up.

Months 7-12: You've now met 12+ experts in your space and earned a trusted reputation with all of them.

Year 2+: Your network grows, your reputation grows, your trust grows. Before you know it, you're the one giving advice to the next generation.

This isn't theory. This is exactly what happened to Brian Chesky with Airbnb. That one relationship - maintained over time, deepened strategically - unlocked an opportunity that became worth $75 billion.

And even if your relationships never lead to Y Combinator or IPOs, you can be confident that they'll give you the one thing we all need: Trust in an age when that essential ingredient is awfully hard to come by.

THE POWER OF FELLOWSHIP IN THE AI AGE

Remember this key point: The ultimate irony of the AI revolution is that human relationships aren't suddenly less important - they're now **more important than ever.**

When AI can match technical skills, your network becomes your moat.

When algorithms can do the work, your relationships determine who gets the opportunity.

When everything online might be fake, your real world tribe's recommendations become the only trusted signal.

The professionals who thrive in the AI age won't just be the ones with the best human skills. They'll be the ones with the best human *networks.*

That's because, unlike the AI that's based on 30-year old neural network techniques, you're building on top of the algorithm that's worked for humans for 300,000 years.

And unlike technical skills that become obsolete, relationships compound in value over time. Every conversation you have this month could be the one that changes your career five years from now.

That's the power of fellowship.

But here's the thing: All these relationships – all this trust you've built, all these connections you've made – they're not just for having interesting conversations over coffee.

They're your competitive advantage when you need opportunities most.

Because while everyone else is still mass-applying to hundreds of jobs online and hoping for the best, you're going to leverage everything you've built to land opportunities that never even get posted.

While other candidates are struggling to get past automated screeners, you're going to have actual humans vouching for you.

And while your competition is trying to fake their way through interviews with AI-generated answers, you're going to show up as the real deal - the person everyone already wants to work with.

That's what Part 3 is all about. Not just building skills and relationships, but **using them strategically** to get your next job, succeed in that job, and even create your own opportunities when traditional employment isn't enough.

So if you're ready to stop playing by the old rules and start making the new ones work for you...

Turn the page. Let's get you hired.

PART 3

WHAT TO DO ABOUT IT NEXT

7

HOW TO GET YOUR NEXT JOB

I went from teaching kindergarten in Brooklyn to working at Apple, LinkedIn, and Google in Silicon Valley.

But it didn't happen overnight.

In fact, it took me seven years of failed applications, ignored resumes, and "thanks but no thanks" emails before I finally broke through.

Seven years.

But here's the thing: It didn't *have* to be that way.

See, I loved teaching my students about technology. Watching their eyes light up when they discovered that computers weren't magic - that they were tools they could actually control and create with.

And I knew that the companies building these tools needed people who understood how real humans (not just engineers) actually learned and used technology.

So I applied. And applied. And applied.

And got rejected. Again. And again. And again.

The problem wasn't a lack of passion - after all, I had been a tech nerd since getting my first DOS-based computer in the early 90s. Or even a dearth of skills - since I was already doing the very things (running a blog, organizing online campaigns) that I would later do in Silicon Valley.

What I didn't have - what took me seven years to figure out - was the fundamental insight that changed everything:

Even in the tech world, hiring is all about people.

Not websites. Not technical skills. Not even pedigrees.

People.

Which means the key skill you need isn't technical. It's human.

It's **empathy.**

The ability to understand what other people need, want, and care about. The ability to see the world through their eyes and give them what they're looking for - whether they're a screener, a recruiter, or a hiring manager.

Once I finally understood this - once I stopped thinking about the job search as a technical problem to solve and started thinking about it as a human problem - everything changed.

Suddenly I was getting responses. Getting interviews. Getting offers.

Not because I got smarter or more qualified. But because I learned to speak to what each person in the hiring process actually cared about.

And that skill - that empathy - is more powerful than ever in the Age of AI.

THE 4 AUDIENCES YOU MUST UNDERSTAND

When I first started trying to land a tech job, I made the same mistake most job seekers make: I thought there was one audience (employers) with one goal (hire the best candidate).

Wrong.

There are actually four distinct audiences you need to win over, each with completely different goals, incentives, and decision-making processes:

1. **The Screener** (The Filter)
2. **The Sourcer** (The Searcher)
3. **The Recruiter** (The Gatekeeper)
4. **The Hiring Manager** (The Decision-Maker)

So in order to develop empathy for each of these audiences, let's take a deep dive into what they need to do their jobs - and what they need from you.

AUDIENCE 1: THE SCREENER

The first person you need to win over isn't the Recruiter or the Hiring Manager. It's someone most job seekers don't even know exists: The Screener.

When I started applying to tech jobs, I didn't understand this. So I'd sharpen my existing teaching resume until it gleamed. I'd craft these beautiful, heartfelt cover letters about my passion for technology. And then I'd apply to 20 jobs.

Crickets.

So I'd apply to 20 more.

Still nothing.

It was like my applications were disappearing into a black hole.

That's because, in a sense, they were.

Understanding the Screener's World

Here's what I eventually figured out: Most companies - especially large ones - have entry-level recruiting coordinators whose entire job is initial screening.

That's because they're dealing with so many hires across so many teams that the number of resumes and candidates becomes astronomical. And so they hire Screeners to spend hours reviewing resumes in Applicant Tracking Systems (ATS), looking at hundreds of candidates every day with one primary goal:

Quickly sort the candidates who meet the essential qualifications from those who don't.

Think about their typical day:

- 600 applications for a new posting came in overnight
- The Recruiter needs to present the top candidates to the Hiring Manager by Friday - which means they need the qualified candidates by end of day
- The Screener has 2 hours blocked off to screen all the applications - which means they're spending 12 seconds per application, on average

So contrary to my initial assumptions, they weren't poring over my heartfelt cover letter. Nor were they carefully evaluating my teacherly accomplishments. Instead, they were doing the same thing that EMTs do - rapid triage into a handful of categories:

1. **Pass along immediately**: You *clearly* can do this job → Send to Recruiter
2. **Hold for review**: You *might* be able to do it → Review again if more candidates are needed
3. **Automatic rejection**: You don't appear *obviously* qualified → Black hole time!

Which meant they were also using technological shortcuts to quickly separate the qualified candidates from the unqualified masses. Specifically, they relied upon scoring algorithms inside the ATS that could immediately measure your fit with the role and sort candidates accordingly (see Figure 7.1):

*Figure 7.1 - How Applicant Tracking Systems
Score and Rank Candidates*

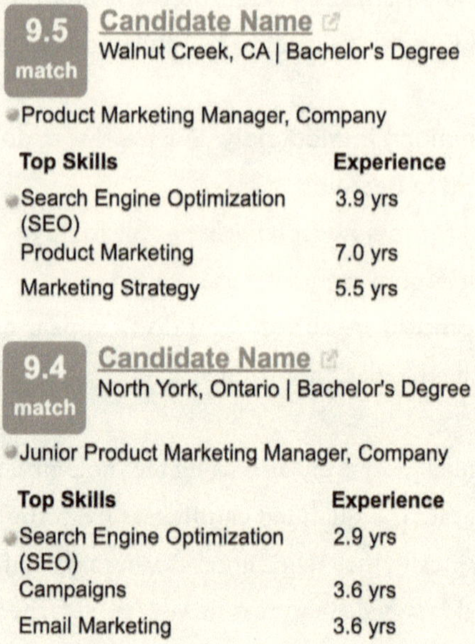

9.5
match
<u>Candidate Name</u>
Walnut Creek, CA | Bachelor's Degree

Product Marketing Manager, Company

Top Skills	Experience
Search Engine Optimization (SEO)	3.9 yrs
Product Marketing	7.0 yrs
Marketing Strategy	5.5 yrs

9.4
match
<u>Candidate Name</u>
North York, Ontario | Bachelor's Degree

Junior Product Marketing Manager, Company

Top Skills	Experience
Search Engine Optimization (SEO)	2.9 yrs
Campaigns	3.6 yrs
Email Marketing	3.6 yrs

*ATS platforms are super simple - does your resume
list the skills and experiences requested on the job
description? If so, your score goes up. If not, sayonora!*

And so once I understood that Screeners were under massive time pressure and needed to identify fit in mere seconds, I completely changed my approach.

Here's What I Did

Step 1: I analyzed job descriptions to understand the exact signals Screeners and the ATS algorithm were looking for

I collected 20 job descriptions for roles I wanted and looked for patterns:

- Which specific skills appeared in nearly every description?
- Which responsibilities were consistently mentioned?
- Which terms were used to describe success in the role?

Again and again, I came across keywords like:

- "Cross-functional collaboration"
- "Stakeholder management"
- "Data-driven decision making"
- "Program evaluation"

Unfortunately, none of those appeared on my teaching resume:

- Taught reading, writing, and math to 25 students
- Worked with parents and administrators on student progress
- Used test scores to improve lesson plans
- Evaluated new curriculum materials

Step 2: I translated my experience into the exact language that Screeners and the algorithm needed to see

Even though none of those precise terms were on my resume, I realized that I'd actually done *all* of those things as a teacher - I just hadn't called them that.

So I went back and re-wrote my bullet points to speak a language that Screeners would understand:

- **Collaborated cross-functionally** with administrators, parents, and peers to align learning objectives and drive measurable improvements
- **Managed competing stakeholder priorities** by building relationships with students, parents, and school leadership
- **Implemented data-driven decision making** by analyzing weekly assessment data to identify learning gaps and adjust instructional strategies
- **Led program evaluation** of new literacy curriculum by tracking effectiveness metrics across 6-month pilot

Same experiences. Different language. And now both the Screener and the ATS could immediately see the signals they sought.

Step 3: I made myself an Obvious Candidate

But even with updated language, I was still at the mercy of what Screeners actually *saw*. Because after making it through the ATS algorithm, the Screener could easily glance at my resume and think: "This guy doesn't *look* like our usual hires."

As such, I also made bolder changes to the top of my resume to make myself look more like an Obvious Candidate - i.e., the kind of person who automatically made sense in just a few seconds.

That included leading with a clear Headline that spoke directly to the exact job title they were looking to fill. And a tight Summary that positioned me as ready to hit the ground running:

Figure 7.2 - Preview of Jeremy's Resume

Jeremy Schifeling **EdTech Program Manager**	123 Main St. | Anytown, CA 90210 123-456-7890 | email@domain.com
Summary	
Experienced education leader with a track record of delivering results in and out of the classroom	

When in doubt, just lead with the exact things your Screener is looking for - the job they need to fill and the experience they need to choose you.

Here's What You Should Do Now

Today, you have a massive advantage I didn't have in 2005: **You have AI.** So when it comes time to translate your resume into the language of Screeners and ATS algorithms, here are some major shortcuts to get you pointed in the right direction quickly.

Step 1: Use AI to identify the most important keywords

Start by asking AI for a list of the critical keywords that your resume will be screened against:

PROMPT

What are the 15 most important skill keywords for this job: [enter job/job description]?

AI OUTPUT

Here are **15 strong, high-value skill keywords** commonly expected for a **Product Manager** role. These work well for resumes, LinkedIn profiles, and job applications:

Top 15 Product Manager Skill Keywords

1. **Product Strategy**

2. **Roadmapping**

3. **User Research**

4. **Product Requirements (PRDs)**

5. **Market Analysis**

There's no need to guess the most important keywords - employers list them right in the job description. And since every AI model has been trained on millions of job descriptions, let AI do the heavy lifting of finding the most important keyword patterns across companies!

Note that you can optimize your resume for a category of jobs (e.g., Program Manager) or a specific job description (e.g., EdTech Program Manager at Apple).

In general, I recommend starting with a resume that's category-specific and then customizing for specific jobs when they're especially appealing. But if you want to get really fancy, you can paste in multiple preferred job descriptions to identify the patterns across those roles.

Just make sure that you avoid the biggest Screener "No-No" of all: Applying with a one-size, fits-all resume. As should be painfully obvious by now, the Screener doesn't have the time, energy, or inclination to figure out why your *generic* resume matches their *specific* job. So, at the very least, have a specific version of your resume for every single category of job you want to pursue.

Step 2: Have AI help you translate your experience into that language

Once you have a list of the most important keywords, you need to make sure that you get credit for as many as you qualify for - in the exact language of the Screener.

So pick things up by uploading your existing resume with this prompt:

PROMPT

Which of those keywords are missing from my resume (see attached)?

For each one that's missing, look through my resume and, if applicable, recommend one bullet point where I can naturally get credit for that keyword.

For each of these bullet points, suggest a revised bullet that incorporates the keyword - but make sure that it doesn't exaggerate or hallucinate what I did and keep it in my existing style.

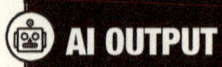 **AI OUTPUT**

> **1. User Research**
>
> **Best location:** Khan Academy — Director, Marketing
> You improved onboarding flows — a perfect place to add user insights.
>
> **Original bullet:**
> "Overhauled onboarding flows via rigorous A/B testing, leading to a 38% increase in our most valuable bottom-of-the-funnel conversions"
>
> **Revised bullet:**
> "Overhauled onboarding flows by pairing user research with rigorous A/B testing, leading to a 38% increase in our most valuable bottom-of-the-funnel conversions"

Notice that a tiny tweak makes a massive difference - just by adding "user research" into the bullet, we now get filtered in instead of filtered out.

Just keep in mind **three essential rules** for success at this stage:

1. **You don't need to match 100% of keywords.**

   While it might seem like a higher match rate is always better, it turns out that perfectly qualified candidates can be problematic (see Figure 7.3). That's because someone who matches every single keyword is likely overqualified, meaning they're less likely to accept the role if offered. Whereas, a merely qualified candidate is likely to be hungrier and more willing to accept - the key result at the end of the day. And the proof is in the data: When Talent Works tested the relationship between qualification rate and interview rate, there was no meaningful difference between a candidate who matched 50% of the qualifications and someone who matched 100%.[73]

Figure 7.3 - Why Matching 50% of Job Requirements Is Enough to Get an Interview

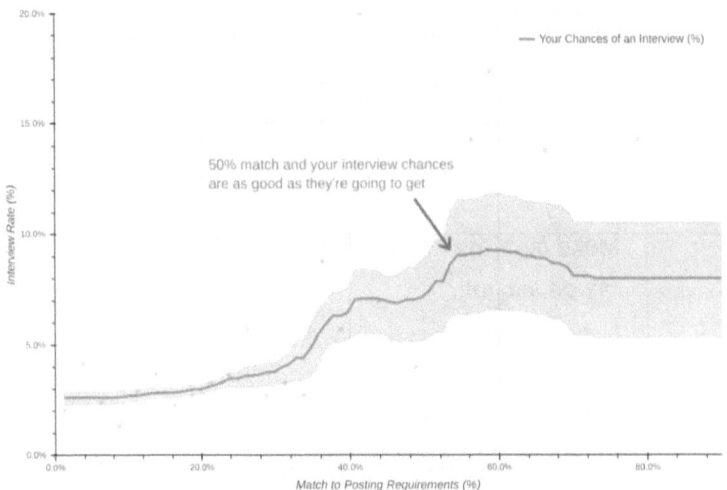

While recruiters might want to bring in someone who's 100% qualified - they also need to find someone who will actually accept the offer. Which means 50%+ qualified is the sweet spot!

---

73   McClear, Sheila. "Study: You Only Need to Be 50% Qualified to Land a Job Interview." *The Ladders*, December 6, 2018. https://www.theladders.com/career-advice/study-you-only-need-to-be-50-qualified-to-land-a-job-interview.

2. **Avoid the temptation to copy-and-paste your AI-generated bullets.**

   I know - no one enjoys writing and rewriting their resume bullets. So I totally understand the temptation to just copy-and-paste your new bullets straight into your resume. And yet, imagine this scenario: Your AI-generated bullets get you past the ATS, past the Screener, even past the Recruiter. And now you're sitting down for a final interview with your future boss - AKA the Hiring Manager. That's when she asks you: "Tell me about this amazing accomplishment on your resume…" - and you realize the whole thing is a giant hallucination… #doh. Like I said, read every single word carefully before adding to your resume!

3. **Make sure the keywords show up in your *Experience* section.**

   Generations of job-seekers have been led to believe that a keyword is a keyword is a keyword. That's why so many job-seekers just dump them in their Skills section - or worse yet, fall prey to the urban legend that they can just encode them in white font! C'mon - let's give the ATS designers a little credit here, people. Because these are expensive tools that often cost more than $100K/year, they've been designed to pull out the most talented candidates - not just the most talented fakers. Which means they screen for keywords in-context - by assessing the length of your skill usage in the context of your Experience section, not just by giving you a binary checkmark for sneaking it in there. So bottom line: Be sure to add your most important keywords to your Experience section, not just your Game-the-System-with-White-Font section (see Figure 7.4)!

Figure 7.4 - How ATS Systems Measure Skill Depth Using Experience, Not Keywords Alone

Forget gaming the system by keyword-stuffing. Instead, showcase your expertise where it actually matters: Right in your Experience section!

Step 3: Make yourself into an Obvious Candidate

The final step is the easiest but most important of all: Let the Screener know you're focused on the same role they are by leading with that on your resume.

All you have to do is grab my resume template from your Surf Kit (available for free at THEJOBINSIDERS.COM/SURF). Once you've got a copy, you can customize both your Headline and your Summary to let Screeners know they've come to the right place.

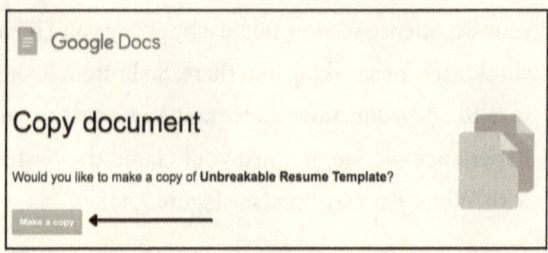

*A one-click resume template: the easiest way to stop
fighting formatting and start shipping applications.*

The other benefit is that my template is already optimized for
both the ATS and the Screener.

Whereas many fancy templates deliver information in ways that
ATS platforms can't handle (e.g., tables, charts, QR codes), mine
will still get all your key points across even if it's compressed into
plain text during the analysis process.

At the same time, it's still appealing for the human Screener's eyes.
Unlike so many templates that cram as much text into a single page
at the expense of readability, mine has ample font sizes and white
space. Because, believe it or not, employers don't actually want a
one-page resume that feels like reading an eye chart (see Figure
7.5). Indeed, when actually offered the option of one vs. two-page
versions in real-world experiments, they almost always prefer the
two-page version.[74] Likely because, after reading hundreds of resumes
with 8-point font and .25" margins, our eyes could all use a break!

---

74 Yang, Peter. "Survey: How Long Should a Resume Be?" *ResumeGo*, accessed
November 13, 2025. https://www.resumego.net/research/one-or-two-page-
resumes/.

Figure 7.5 - Hiring Rate: Two-Page vs One-Page Resumes

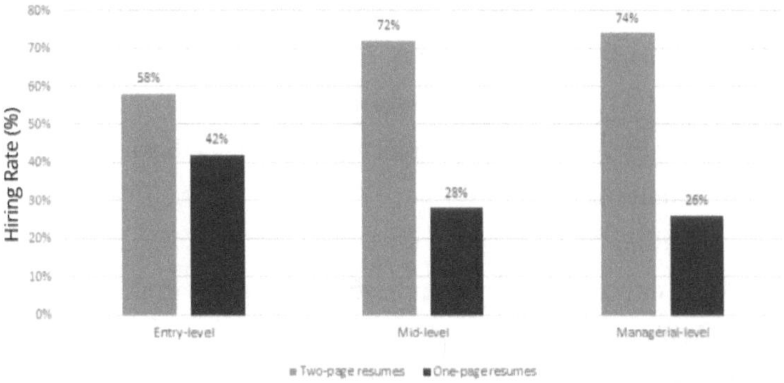

One of the most surprising findings in the annals of job-searching - and a powerful reminder to avoid conventional wisdom and seek data instead.

AUDIENCE 2: THE SOURCER

As important as the Screener is, it turns out there are actually *two* ways to get to the next step of the hiring process:

1. The Screener reviews your inbound application and passes you to the Recruiter.
2. The Sourcer goes out into the world to find you and recommends you to the Recruiter.

And when I finally figured this out, it changed everything about my job search.

Understanding the Sourcer's World

Here's what I didn't know when I was desperately applying to hundreds of tech jobs: There was an entire parallel universe of hiring out there - and I was completely invisible in that universe.

That universe?

LinkedIn.

And I only really came to understand it once I started working at LinkedIn myself.

But you don't have to work at LinkedIn to understand its importance. Here's a crash course on the three main reasons that companies proactively *search* for candidates - in addition to reactively reviewing the ones that come to them:

1. The best candidates often aren't applying

Top performers are usually happily employed. They're not browsing job boards or submitting applications. But they might be open to the right opportunity if someone reached out to them directly. These "passive candidates" are the Holy Grail of recruiting - and the only way to reach them is through outbound sourcing.

2. Application volume ≠ application quality

Just because 600 people applied doesn't mean 600 *qualified* people applied. Often, companies get flooded with applications from people who are nowhere close to qualified. Meanwhile, the perfect candidate might not even know the role exists. Sourcers solve this problem by going out and finding exactly who they need.

3. The AI application tsunami

Remember what we talked about earlier - how AI makes it easy for everyone to spam employers with bogus applications? Companies have noticed. And they're responding by relying MORE on outbound sourcing and LESS on inbound applications. Especially since the research shows that people are less likely to lie on their LinkedIn profiles than their resumes, given the public nature of the former.[75]

So that's why companies rely upon Sourcers.

But what do they actually do?

To understand Sourcers' work, you need to understand their most important tool: LinkedIn Recruiter.

Figure 7.6 - Preview of LinkedIn Recruiter Tool

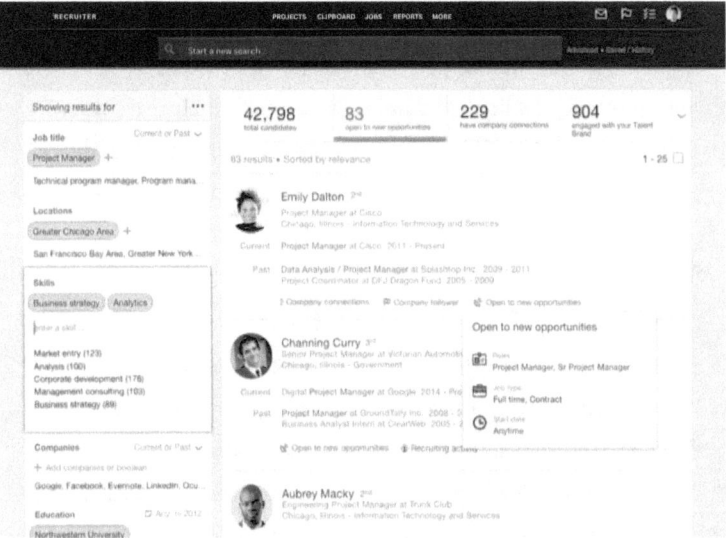

The $10K/year version of LinkedIn that gives employers access to over 1 billion profiles!

---

75 Guillory, Jamie, and Jeffrey T. Hancock. 2012. "The Effect of LinkedIn on Deception in Resumes." *Cyberpsychology, Behavior, and Social Networking* 15 (3): 135-139. https://socialmedialab.sites.stanford.edu/sites/g/files/sbiybj22976/files/media/file/guillory-cbsn-linkedin.pdf.

Just like the ATS used by a Screener, LinkedIn Recruiter gives the Sourcer access to a wide range of candidates. But unlike an ATS, which only collects people who explicitly apply for roles, LinkedIn Recruiter gives the Sourcer access to every single professional in the world - over 1.3 billion at last count.

So the essence of the Sourcer's work is filtering out the vast, vast majority of LinkedIn users to leave behind just the professionals who fit a specific role. Which means your job is to make sure that you show up on their screen - and make it easy for them to choose you.

Here's What I Did

Once I understood how Sourcers actually worked, I realized my LinkedIn profile was massively inadequate. Even though I might have been a strong candidate, I'd never show up on their searches since I'd built a generic profile - not one that was specific to their filters.

So I systematically rebuilt my profile to start showing up.

Step 1: I started with my Headline

One of the first things I realized about Sourcers and their LinkedIn Recruiter tool is that they both have tough jobs to do.

LinkedIn Recruiter has to search through over a billion candidates and return just the top matches - and then the Sourcer has to choose the very best from that group in minutes, not hours.

And then on top of that, they both have to deal with candidates who are trying to game the system - stuffing all these keywords into their profile to make sure they turn up for lots of different jobs.

So where do both of them start this epic task?

With the Headline - that little piece of text that sits beneath your name.

Behold, the LinkedIn Headline: Small, but mighty!

That's because the Headline is the hardest part of your profile to game. Unlike your Experience or Skills sections, you can't just stuff hundreds of keywords in there. After all, it's limited to 220 characters - shorter even than a Tweet.

Therefore, Sourcers and the LinkedIn Recruiter algorithm tend to see it as a more authentic signal - giving it more weight in both the results and their picks. And you can see this for yourself in the screenshot below, where the exact job title the Sourcer searches for shows up in the Headlines of all the top-rated candidates:

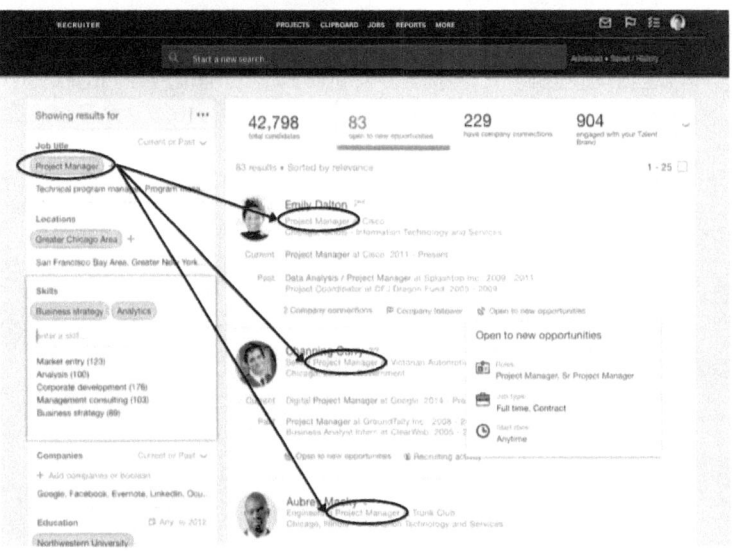

The Recruiter search results view: If your Headline doesn't match what they're looking for, you simply don't exist.

Which meant that I couldn't just focus on the past with a Headline like "Kindergarten Teacher." Instead, I had to tell Sourcers where I was headed by nailing my most important keyword in my most important section: "Exploring EdTech Program Manager Roles."

Note that I *didn't* claim to be something I wasn't - but I also didn't rely on magical thinking: Maybe Sourcers can read my mind and figure out what I can do for them?

Instead, I gave them a clear path forward - and put myself on their radars for the very first time.

Step 2: I copied my resume bullets into my Experience

But the Headline alone wasn't enough. Even though I was now on the LinkedIn Recruiter radar, I was competing with 10,000 other candidates who also had "EdTech Program Manager" in their Headlines.

To separate myself from the pack, I realized that I also needed to match the specific skills the Sourcer was looking for - just like the Screener did with the ATS:

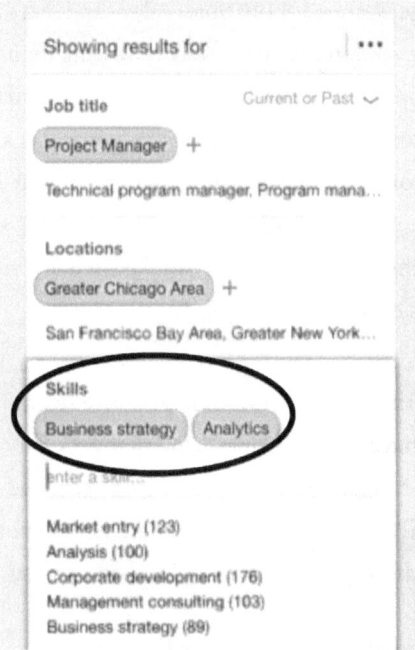

*Once employers filter for job title, they quickly move on
to Skills. In other words, can you walk the talk?*

But rather than reinvent the wheel, I simply copied over all the bullet points from my resume straight into my LinkedIn Experience section. Because one of the things I realized while working at LinkedIn is that the vast majority of professionals don't realize that profiles need to be just as complete as resumes.

Why?

It's simple math:

- Even if you apply to 100 jobs a day with your resume, the absolute maximum number of times your resume will get scanned is **100 times a day** - and that's assuming that ever Screener is actively reviewing their ATS

- On the other hand, even if you haven't updated your LinkedIn profile in a year, it's getting scanned **50 million times a day** (since there are about 1 million recruiters on LinkedIn, each averaging about 50 searches a day - and every LinkedIn Recruiter search scans every single profile)[76]

So given that massive difference in attention, I realized it's madness to have a thorough resume that gets attention once in a while - and a blank LinkedIn profile that's scanned constantly.

And so I filled up my LinkedIn Experience section with all the most important keywords, just like I did on my resume.

Step 3: I let Sourcers know I was in the game

But even after nailing the Headline and Experience sections, I was still competing with 1,000 other candidates who had both the right focus and the right skills.

So to stand out against more experienced candidates, I had to help the Sourcer solve a fundamental challenge: Even when they pay $10,000 a year for access to LinkedIn Recruiter, they're still at the mercy of LinkedIn's arbitrary InMail limits.

---

76 Tegze, Jan. "LinkedIn 2024: Asia & Africa Recruiters Surge, Europe & South America Decline." LinkedIn, 2025. https://www.linkedin.com/pulse/ linkedin-2024-asia-africa-recruiters-surge-europe-south-jan-tegze-94p0c/.

Just like we mere mortals get a measly 5 monthly InMails (messages to people we're not connected with on the platform) when we shell out for LinkedIn Premium, even the most expensive LinkedIn Recruiter account includes just 150 InMails per month. Which isn't nearly enough if you've got 1,000 candidates to consider for a single role.

The reason LinkedIn can get away with both these outrageous prices and these strict limits is that it's basically a monopoly. In other words, if you're a Sourcer and want access to all of the world's professional talent, where else can you even look?

Exactly.

But before you accuse LinkedIn of being absolutely cold-hearted, keep in mind that the recruiting world drives 60% of all its revenue - so it does have to throw Sourcers a little bone.[77] Specifically, it makes them the following offer that no Sourcer can refuse:

- If you send InMails to candidates who never respond, that's *bad* for everyone. You wasted your InMail, the candidate feels spammed, and LinkedIn's brand is tarnished as a place no one wants to go. So to punish you for choosing poorly, you've now lost that InMail credit for the rest of the month.

- On the other hand, if you send an InMail to a candidate who does respond, that's *great* for everyone. You

---

77   LeadCRM, "How Does LinkedIn Make Money? (A Look At Its 4 Revenue Streams)," LeadCRM (blog), last modified June 5, 2024, accessed November 15, 2025, https://www.leadcrm.io/blog/how-does-linkedin-make-money.

unearthed an awesome candidate, our user feels thrilled to have an opportunity fall into their lap, and LinkedIn is starting to look better and better for all parties. So to reward you for choosing wisely, **we're going to give you that InMail credit back**, so you can continue to reach out to more wise choices.

Capisce?

Now, a really savvy Sourcer can extend their InMail budget indefinitely by ensuring they only reach out to candidates who are extremely likely to respond.

But how do they do that?

Through the magic of LinkedIn Recruiter's engagement filters:

*Have too many candidates and too little
time? Just filter for engagement!*

Unlike the filters on the left side of the screen that more closely match the ATS filters (job title, location, skills, education), these filters leverage the unique signals generated by LinkedIn users to forecast who's most likely to respond to Sourcer outreach.

These include:

- **Open to New Opportunities:** Are you actually open to a new job - or are you perfectly content in your current role?

- **Company Connections:** Do you know someone at our firm - or are you a total stranger?
- **Engaged with Your Talent Brand:** Are you showing specific interest in our firm - or just in getting a new job in general?
- **InMail Response Rate:** Do you actually respond to InMails - or is your lack of response costing sourcers their precious credits?

Note that this last one isn't actually shown on the screen since LinkedIn applies it automatically by pushing up candidates with a high response rate and driving down those with a low reply rate. After all, Sourcers are LinkedIn's Golden Goose, so they definitely want to ensure that they have a good experience and don't waste InMails on non-responding deadbeats!

And so here's what I did to make sure I got filtered in - instead of filtered out:

- **Open to New Opportunities:** I turned on the Open to Work signal on my profile to let Sourcers know I was in the game. This not only got me filtered in but also let me cover the different roles and locations I was interested in:

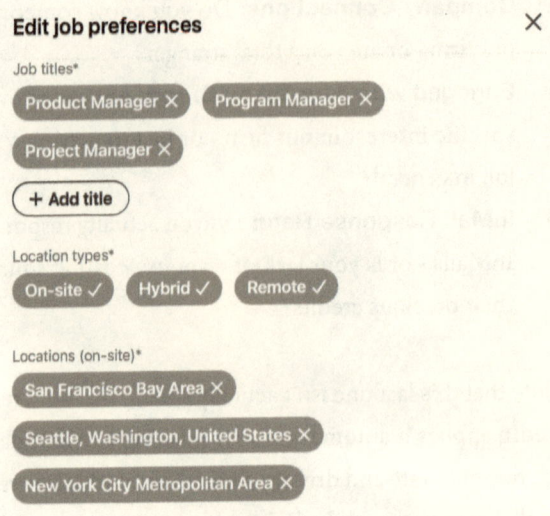

- But note: I definitely didn't want my current boss finding out, so I made sure to turn on the Recruiters Only version of the signal. That way, Sourcers at other companies could find me - but the Sourcers at my own company wouldn't rat me out to my boss!

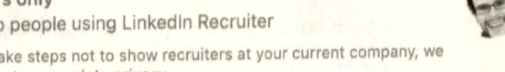

Send the right signals to the right people - and no one else!

- **Company Connections:** To demonstrate my connection to the companies I was most excited about, I made sure to get credit on LinkedIn for all the connections I had in real life. That's because I noticed that lots of my past classmates and colleagues had moved on to work for some of the coolest companies. And so just by connecting with them on LinkedIn, I could show the algorithm and the Sourcer I had an "In" at just about every company.

- **Engaged with Your Talent Brand:** This was the easiest filter to master. All I did was spend a rainy Saturday afternoon "Following" the LinkedIn pages of every single company I liked. And voila - just like that, I was getting filtered in instead of out:

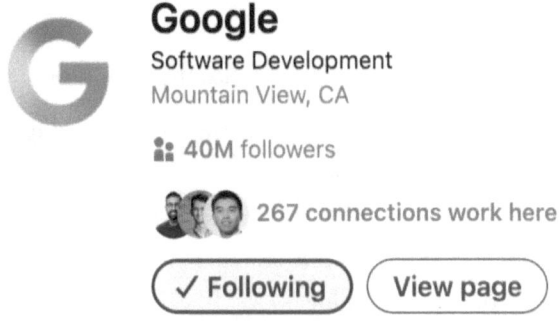

A single click is the difference between being filtered in and out!

- **InMail Response Rate:** This, on the other hand, was the hardest one to wrap my head around. Even though I had spent the first decade of my online life avoiding Spam like the plague, now I engaged with it to teach the LinkedIn Recruiter algorithm that I was plugged-in and responsive. But just to be clear, I wasn't pretending to show interest - just politely declining right away to make sure that the algorithm could tell I had a pulse:

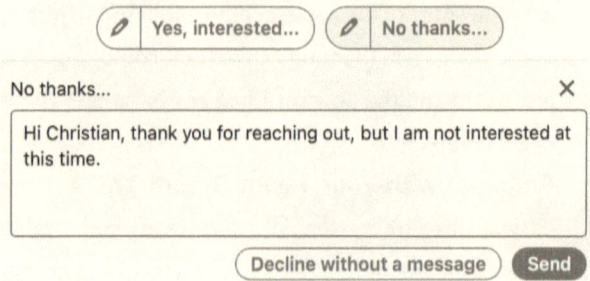

What's the strongest predictor of your likelihood to respond to the next InMail? Your response to the last InMail, of course. So respond accordingly!

Step 4: I won over the human - not just the algorithm

At this point, I had done a pretty thorough job of proving my fit to the LinkedIn Recruiter algorithm:

- I matched the job title search in my most important section, the Headline
- I matched the Skills search in my Experience
- I matched the engagement filters from my Open to Work section all the way to my InMail response rate

And yet, I still had to win over the most important algorithm of all - that's right, the Human Algorithm.

Because as discussed in the last chapter, humans aren't as motivated by keywords or online switches - but by the natural signals we've evolved to care about over millennia.

So to win over that Human Algorithm, I thought about the four things that every human cares about:

1. **Visuals:** We've been a visual species for much longer than we've been a literate species. So naturally, we prefer looking at images over reading text - and the same is true for LinkedIn profiles. That's why your Cover Photo is so important. It's not just the first thing the Sourcer sees; it's also the only large visual asset on the entire page.

2. **Faces:** What do we love looking at best? Each other. Even newborn babies show a preference for gazing at faces over everything else.[78] So it's no surprise that LinkedIn profiles with a Profile Photo get 21X more views than those without them.[79] But it's not just the face that matters - it's what's on it. Which is why Sourcers look for the same signals our ancestors looked for: A genuine smile from a potential friend? Or a fake smile from a potential foe?

3. **Stories:** What's our species' secret for sharing complicated information across thousands of generations and billions of people? Stories. Our tales have survived for

78 Poles, Karol, Irene Ronga, and Francesca Garbarini. "At First Sight: The Prenatal Origins of Face Recognition." *International Congress of Infant Studies Baby Blog*, April 17 2025. Accessed November 16 2025. https://infantstudies. org/at-first-sight-the-prenatal-origins-of-face-recognition/.

79 LinkedIn Sales Solutions. "Picture Perfect: Make a Great First Impression with Your LinkedIn Profile." *LinkedIn Business – Sales Blog*. Accessed November 16, 2025. https://www.linkedin.com/business/sales/blog/b2b-sales/ picture-perfect--make-a-great-first-impression-with-your-linkedi.

millennia not just by being fun - but by being sticky. That's why Stanford research shows that we're 22X more likely to remember a story than a simple fact.[80] And that's why Sourcers love a well-told About section - because it's the best story on your profile.

4. **Trust:** And finally, as Chapter 6 made clear - the last vestige of trust in our AI age isn't from algorithms or keywords; it's from people. Which is why LinkedIn Recommendations are so much more important than Endorsements. While the latter provides little information about the context of the relationship (is the Endorser your mom?) and even less about the strength of the testimonial (is this person amazing at this skill - or merely proficient?), the former provides rich detail on both counts. Which explains why Recommendations are featured prominently in LinkedIn Recruiter - and Endorsements aren't mentioned at all.

And then I upgraded each of those components in turn:

1. **Visuals:** I found a gorgeous - and free - whiteboard photo from PEXELS.COM that represented both Program Management and Education. And then I brought it over to Canva to further emphasize my positioning. Voila - instant Cover Photo and visual gold:

---

80 Aaker, Jennifer. "Harnessing the Power of Stories." VMware Women's Leadership Innovation Lab, Stanford University. Accessed November 16 2025. https://womensleadership.stanford.edu/resources/voice-influence/ harnessing-power-stories.

EdTech Program Manager

Nail the visual AND your positioning in one fell swoop!

2. **Faces:** My original Profile Photo was shot from about 100 feet away where you could barely see my face. So I snapped a selfie with my best Duchenne Smile (a genuine smile that activates autonomic nervous system muscles like dimpling in the cheeks and wrinkling around the corners of the eyes) - vs. the fake Botox Smile (smiling only in the teeth, not the rest of the face) that suggests you can't be trusted. And then I ran it through Snappr's free Photo Analyzer (all links in your Surf Kit) to make sure my I was sending the right signals:

Jeremy's Photo Score:

79/100

You've done pretty well. But there's always room for improvement, so check out our very actionable tips below.

Share your score

or upload another photo to analyze

Even career book authors have room to improve!

3. **Stories:** My first About section was basically about…
    nothing. That's because it was just a bunch of random
    facts from across my career - the very thing that our
    human brains process *out*. So to make it stick, I wove
    those facts into a coherent story:

About

All my life, I've been passionate about education and technology. From helping
kindergarteners learn to use computers in Bed-Stuy, Brooklyn to bringing tech-powered
mentoring to millions of young people around the world at iMentor, I love nothing more than
seeing others succeed - at scale.

And that's why I'm thrilled to bring my expertise and passion to the world of EdTech.
Because the biggest obstacle in EdTech is to bridge these two worlds, to get technology to
speak the language of education. And having worked at this intersection for over seven
years, I can't wait to apply my skills towards the toughest challenges and to serve the most
students.

Want to win over your audience? Do the same thing
all great communicators do - tell a story.

4. **Trust:** Finally, to prove that I was as qualified as I
    claimed, I needed to get some 3rd-party validation of
    my abilities. That meant reaching out to former bosses
    and clients to get Recommendations like so:

Emily Metcalf · 2nd
Program and Project Management | Operations Senior Leader | Government Policy
and Administration
July 23, 2010, Emily was Jeremy's client

Jeremy provided exceptional service and support in my work with his company,
iMentor. At client meetings he made our team feel comfortable with the products and
services, and went the extra-mile delivering solutions that fit our needs. He is very
reliable and remained level-headed during times of stress. Jeremy was great to work
with always went out of his way to provide solutions and recommendations.

You saying that you're great: Obviously. An objective
3rd party saying so: Recruitment gold!

And after making my profile visible on LinkedIn Recruiter's radar screen and desirable to the Sourcer using it, I began to see the first fruits of my labor in the form of inquiries like the following:

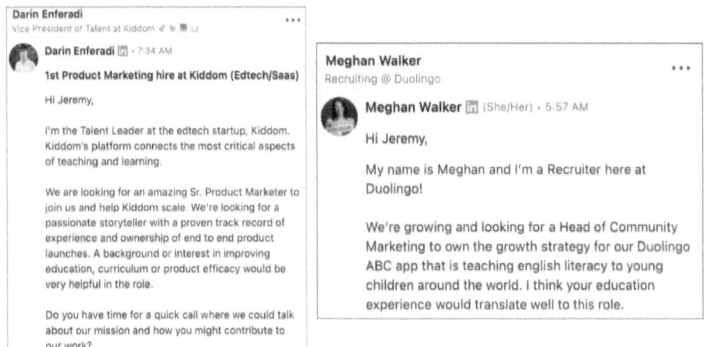

Want to have employers reaching out to you for the rest of your career? Start building a magnetic LinkedIn profile today.

Here's What You Should Do Now

Want to start getting that kind of Sourcer attention yourself? Here are the key Pareto Principle steps to optimize your LinkedIn profile. In other words, notice that they don't focus on every random LinkedIn feature (posting content that has no bearing on Sourcer searches, buying LinkedIn Premium which doesn't change your ranking on the LinkedIn Recruiter screen) - but just the 20% of features that drive 80% of your results.

Step 1: Start with your Headline

Don't overthink this one - just give the LinkedIn Recruiter algorithm and the Sourcer what they want: *The specific job title you can do for them.*

And just as with my example, if you don't have that job title already, you can always couch it in the language of exploration: "Exploring Product Manager Roles" or "Seeking Data Scientist Opportunities."

Finally, to add a little extra oomph to this important section, you can ask AI to comb through your resume to find other supporting material:

 PROMPT

Build a LinkedIn headline that shows my
interest in and fit with [job title] roles
based on my resume: [insert resume]

 AI OUTPUT

Here are several **LinkedIn headline options**
tailored for **Data Science roles**, crafted
to highlight your analytical depth, quantitative MBA background, and data-driven
marketing achievements:

Option 1: Analytical & Professional
MBA | Data-Driven Marketing Leader Pivoting
to Data Science | Proven Expertise in Growth
Analytics, Experimentation & Insights

Option 2: Quantitative & Impact-Focused
Ex-LinkedIn & Apple | Marketing Executive
Turned Data Science Candidate | SQL, Analyt-
ics, and Growth Modeling Expertise

Don't overthink this critical section - get it focused, ASAP.

But what if you're currently employed?

Can you imagine arriving at the office on Monday morning, only to find a printout of your LinkedIn profile on your desk with your new Headline circled in red, and a note from your boss: "Come see me in my office..."

So if you want to let Sourcers know you're in the game without tipping off your boss, just leverage the Open to Work feature. Specifically, list the exact job titles you want to be found for - but make sure to turn on the "Recruiters only" version.

That way, Sourcers at other companies can see and choose you. But neither your current boss nor your own Sourcing team will be able to see the signal. In other words, the very best of both worlds!

Step 2: Copy your resume bullets into your Experience

Just like with the Headline, don't get stuck with Analysis Paralysis when it comes to your LinkedIn profile's Experience section.

The easiest thing to do is copy-and-paste your resume's newly-improved bullet points right in. And you can even grab my template in your Surf Kit to get these nice little bullet point icons to show up on your profile:

LinkedIn
2 yrs 1 mo
San Francisco Bay Area

Senior Product Marketing Manager
2013 - 2014 · 1 yr

▶ Doubled student user base to 39M through social and video marketing - including LinkedIn's most watched video of all time (5M YouTube views)

▶ Consistently delivered record-breaking email campaigns (45% open rate, 15% CTR) that, cumulatively, drove 10M+ site visits

> *How many employers scan your resume on your hard drive everyday? None (unless they've hacked in!). How many scan your LinkedIn profile everyday? Millions. So get those killer bullet points off your resume and onto your profile, pronto.*

But what if you've got multiple resumes - and are pursuing multiple roles?

Unlike with resumes, you've only got a *single* LinkedIn profile to work with - so you've got to make the most of it. And that means drawing upon the power of AI to bridge your different interests with a prompt like this:

 PROMPT

I need to create a single LinkedIn profile that's focused on both [job title 1] and [job title 2]. Can you please take both versions of my resume and combine into a single Experience section that work for both job titles: [paste resume 1] [paste resume 2]

AI OUTPUT

Here's a **unified LinkedIn "Experience" section** that fuses both versions of your resume into one cohesive profile – crafted to resonate equally with **Product Marketing** and **Career Coaching** audiences.

This version keeps a natural LinkedIn tone (not too résumé-like), includes your measurable wins, and embeds critical keywords for both domains: go-to-market strategy, product positioning, content marketing, growth, mentorship, coaching, and professional development.

Experience
Founder & CEO | Product Marketing + Career Strategy Leader

Break into Tech | 2015 - Present | Mountain View, CA

- Founded a career platform helping thousands of professionals – from teachers to consultants – transition into tech roles at companies like Google, LinkedIn, and Spotify.

- Built a community of 90K+ subscribers through content marketing, SEO, and social strategy, all with zero paid ad spend.

- Developed and taught career development and personal branding programs used by Harvard Business School, Stanford GSB, and the Peace Corps.

Want to get the best of two different job worlds in a single profile? Let AI find the hidden connections between those worlds and stitch together a unified profile!

Step 3: Let Sourcers know you're in the game

Once you're showing up on LinkedIn Recruiter, you've got to convince Sourcers that you're InMail-worthy. And that means giving them high confidence that you'll respond to their messages in all of the ways they filter for engagement:

Open to New Opportunities

Make sure you've got Open to Work turned on - both for the jobs and locations you prefer and for the signal you want to send ("Recruiters only" vs. "All LinkedIn members"). While you only need the former to get filtered in on LinkedIn Recruiter, there may be an advantage to choosing the latter.

That's because of the power of "weak ties" - i.e., the hard-to-believe but massively-validated idea that people you only know a little bit are *more likely* to help you find a job than your own friends and family.[81] And so by adding the bold "#OpenToWork" green badge to your Profile Photo, you'll be letting your weak ties (classmates from a decade ago, colleagues from three jobs ago) know that you're in the game. Which is, perhaps, why LinkedIn's own research shows that you're 20% more likely to get messages from your community after turning it on.[82]

And meanwhile, don't sweat all the mythology around the green badge being a "badge of shame." Once you know that Sourcers desperately want you to be clear about your intentions,

81 Dizikes, Peter. "The Power of Weak Ties in Gaining New Employment." *MIT News*, September 15, 2022. https://news.mit.edu/2022/weak-ties-linkedin-employment-0915.

82 Rajiv, Rohan. "To Find Your Next Job More Quickly, Tell Your Community You're Open to Work." *LinkedIn Blog (Member Products)*, October 29, 2020. https://www.linkedin.com/blog/member/product/the-benefits-of-sharing-with-your-community-you-re-open-to-work.

you'll see why it's no wonder that those with the badge are 40% more likely to receive InMails - and that my own survey shows most Sourcers couldn't care less about the debate:[83]

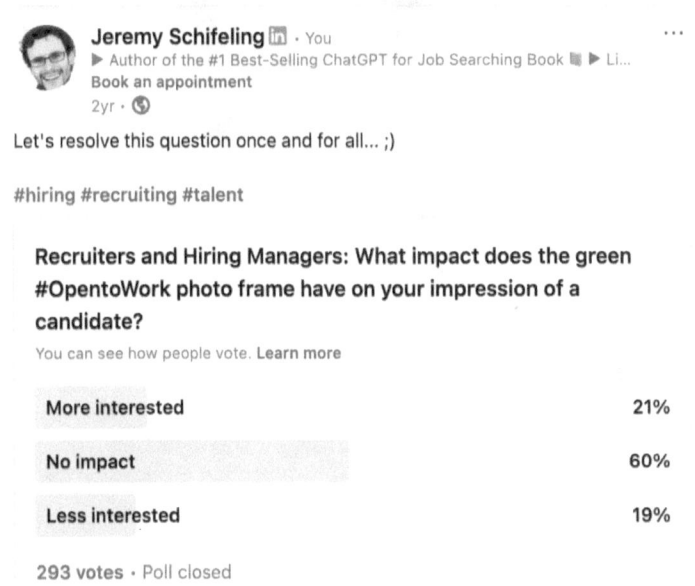

Jeremy Schifeling in · You
▶ Author of the #1 Best-Selling ChatGPT for Job Searching Book ◖ ▶ Li...
Book an appointment
2yr · 🌐

Let's resolve this question once and for all... ;)

#hiring #recruiting #talent

Recruiters and Hiring Managers: What impact does the green #OpentoWork photo frame have on your impression of a candidate?

You can see how people vote. **Learn more**

More interested	21%
No impact	60%
Less interested	19%

293 votes · Poll closed

Ditch the Open to Work shame game: Recruiters
don't care so nor should you.

Company Connections

The next time you've got 10 minutes to spare, head over to LinkedIn's My Network tab - and specifically, the People You May Know section. What you'll discover is that LinkedIn's data scientists are world class at guessing who you already know - especially since there's a good chance that if you and another user know the same people, you'll likely know *each other* too.

---

83   Ibid.

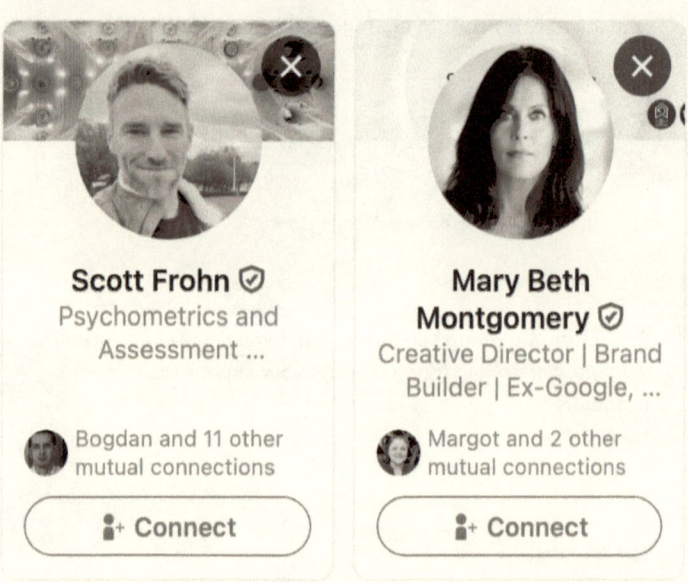

LinkedIn data scientists are scary good at guessing who you already know. Not by being creepers but by relying on Network Theory 101!

So just spending a few minutes clicking "Connect" on all the people you already know will boost your chances in two ways:

1. By ensuring that you get filtered in on the "Company Connections" tab whenever a long-lost connection has moved to a company that's scouting for candidates.

2. By pushing you up in the search results whenever one of your contact's connections is searching.

That's because, all things being equal, LinkedIn knows that 2nd Degree Connections (i.e., a friend of a friend) are more desirable than random strangers.

Engaged with Your Talent Brand

Following LinkedIn Company Pages also just takes minutes - but can be accelerated even further by AI. Instead of thinking up and then manually searching for every interesting company, you can just run this prompt:

PROMPT

```
I'm interested in the following companies:
[List Companies]. Please suggest 50 similar
companies and, for each one, please provide
a direct link to their LinkedIn Company
Page.
```

And now you've got a handy list that makes it as simple as:

1. Click the link
2. Click "Follow"
3. Rinse, wash, and repeat

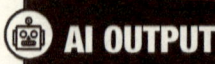

AI OUTPUT

> Here are **50 companies** similar to Khan
> Academy, Duolingo, and Coursera (in the
> EdTech / online learning space). For each,
> a direct link to their LinkedIn company page
> is provided where available.

#	COMPANY	LINKEDIN COMPANY PAGE
1	Udemy	https://www.linkedin.com/company/udemy/
2	edX	https://www.linkedin.com/company/edx/
3	Skillshare	https://www.linkedin.com/company/skillshare/

Don't fall into the Brand Name Job Trap. Just because you've heard of a company doesn't make it a great one to work for (see Enron, FTX, etc.). In fact, non-brand name firms may actually offer better opportunities due to less competition.

InMail Response Rate

Start by going to your LinkedIn inbox and filter for all your old InMails that you may have left lying fallow. Then, just go through and click "No thanks," followed by "Decline without a message" - and voila, your Response Rate just went from nearly 0% to 100%.

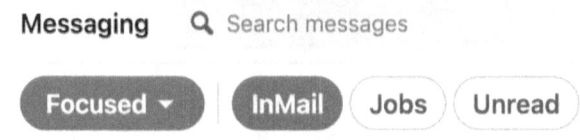

Need to go back and get credit for responding to a bunch of old InMails? Just use the handy "InMail" button in your LinkedIn inbox to do some quick triage!

Now all you've got to do is keep it up for future InMails and you're well on your way to a big boost in your LinkedIn Recruiter standings!

Step 4: Win over the human

But, of course, merely rising to the top of LinkedIn Recruiter isn't enough. Once your profile shows up in a Sourcer's search results, they still need to click on your profile and decide if you're worth reaching out to.

Which means it's time to ace the Human Algorithm:

1. Visuals

Start with a compelling Cover Photo that both captures the Sourcer's visual imagination and aligns with your positioning. And while it might be tempting to use AI, I've found that even state-of-the-art models produce content that's corny at best and just wrong at worst:

These AI-generated photos broadcast "I don't really know AI - but I'm not afraid to use it!"

So skip the hassle and just follow my steps from above:

a. Search PEXELS.COM for royalty-free photos relevant to your desired job (e.g., "data visualization" for Data Scientists or "blueprints" for Architects)

b. Then click the "Edit in Canva" button to bring it over to Canva - which won't require a paid account since we're not using their templates

c. Finally, click Canva's Text button to add in a Heading that makes your positioning crystal-clear:

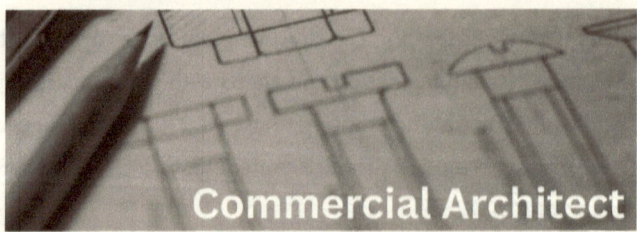

Voila: Focused, engaging, and no spelling errors!

You now have a Cover Photo that's more than a pretty picture - it's a Welcome Mat to the human Sourcer who's looking for someone they can believe in.

2. Faces

Again, skip the temptation to use one of those AI-powered Profile Photo generators. You don't need to spend money to get something that just gives Sourcers that "Uncanny Valley" ick-factor of "almost human but not quite…"

People hire people, not robots. Choose carefully.

Instead, follow these DIY instructions to save your money - and your Sourcer's sanity:

a. Dress in whatever attire best represents the world you want to enter. Because we're a tribal species, don't make yourself an outsider by wearing a three-piece suit if you want a startup job or a hoodie if you want to break into investment banking. Instead, make yourself an insider by dressing like one. And when in doubt, check out the Profile Photos of those who have the jobs you already want as a little visual clue.

b. Make sure you've got that nice Duchenne Smile communicating what a friendly, trustworthy teammate you'll be. Because it relies upon your autonomic nervous system (which is why it's so hard to fake - and why our Human BS detectors trust it more than a Botox Smile), try thinking about something that genuinely makes you smile (like the awesome opportunities that this photo is going to bring you):

Make sure you "Smize" (smile in your eyes). Your teeth aren't enough!

c. Once you're all set-up, take a Portrait Mode selfie with your phone. Just make sure you've got a plain background since the key visual information for the Sourcer is your face, not your cool wallpaper.

d. And then run it through Snappr to see if there's anything else you can do to sharpen the signal you're sending:

Face 93/100

Smile   PERFECT

Jawline   PERFECT

Squinch   GOOD

You're very close. Use those facial muscles just a tad more to get your eyes into a slightly tighter squinch position for a perfect score. **More information**

Gotta work on that Squinch... :)

3. Stories

The About section is the only section on your LinkedIn profile that's truly wide open to tell your story. So tell it well by drawing upon the key components of effective storytelling with this prompt:

PROMPT

Help me write a LinkedIn About section (150-200 words) that:

1. 1. Opens with a compelling hook about my professional focus: [Describe Your Goal]

2. 2. Tells my career story authentically, drawing upon just a few highlights from my resume below

3. 3. Ends with what I'm passionate about or looking for

4. 4. Sounds conversational (like I'm talking directly to my future employer, not a search algorithm)

[insert resume]

AI OUTPUT

I'm working toward one clear goal: becoming the Chief Marketing Officer of an EdTech company that's transforming how people learn.

My path here has been anything but traditional—but that's what makes it powerful. I started in the classroom, teaching kindergarten in Brooklyn, where I learned how deeply education can change a life. That insight guided every step that followed—from helping LinkedIn double its student user base to 39 million (and creating its most-watched video ever) to building a $40M sales pipeline at Fidelis in just two months.

Most recently, I founded Break Into Tech, the first platform helping non-coders land roles at top tech companies. With zero marketing budget, we grew a 10K+ subscriber base and helped clients earn offers from Google, Spotify, and more—all while earning national press coverage.

Now, I'm eager to bring that same mix of data-driven growth, creative storytelling, and mission-driven leadership to an EdTech company that's ready to scale its impact. Because great marketing doesn't just drive metrics—it opens doors for learners everywhere.

A great About section doesn't have to be rocket science - but it should draw upon storytelling science!

Note that this approach to AI-powered writing steers clear of the hallucination problem because it's based on your resume - not just a bunch of arbitrary keywords. But it's still prone to the issue of sounding a little robotic.

So to hold your AI's "feet" to the fire, I encourage you to both revise the section in your own style and then share it with the trusted advisors you engaged with in Chapter 6. By getting some trusted eyes on your About section (and profile more broadly), you can ensure that you're truly ready for LinkedIn primetime!

4. Trust

Speaking of trust, there's no point in building out a world-class LinkedIn profile where the Sourcer just says "Yeah, right - of course *you* think you're awesome!"

So to get that social proof that we humans crave so much, just reach out to a handful of former managers and/or clients for a LinkedIn Recommendation. Ideally, you want someone who had power over *you* - not the other way around - since the Recommendation includes the context of your relationship and Sourcers can sniff out BS testimonials ("I loved working for Jeremy - he's just the world's greatest boss!") from a mile away.

And when you do reach out, be sure to make it easy for them to say "Yes" by jogging their memory and focusing your writing with a message like the following one:

Hi [name],

I'm updating my LinkedIn profile and would love a recommendation from you since we worked together on [specific project/time].

I'm specifically trying to highlight my [specific skill], so if you feel comfortable speaking to that, it would be incredibly helpful.

Happy to write one for you as well!

Thanks,
[your name]

I find that this tit-for-tat approach gets a 90% response rate given that our Human Algorithm is also driven by reciprocity/fairness as well as generosity/generativity.

Just remember that, unlike Endorsements, you don't need hundreds of Recommendations. Even 1-2 really powerful ones are enough to tip the odds in your favor when your competition, like the vast majority of LinkedIn users, has none!

I know that was a long slog through the swamps of LinkedIn but, trust me, it's going to be worth it.

Because you're no longer competing with 600 other applicants inside the ATS or even 1.3 billion other users on LinkedIn. Instead, you'll be one of a handful of candidates the Sourcer reaches out to. **Not just now, but forever.**

Because that's the beauty of LinkedIn - it's your 24/7 resume, earning you opportunities even while you sleep.

And that's the power of empathizing with Sourcers. Because while everyone else is desperately sending out applications into the void, you're getting tapped on the shoulder by companies that actually *want* to hire you.

AUDIENCE 3: THE RECRUITER

Congrats! You've passed one of the first two tests. Either:

1. Your resume stood out in the ATS and got the Screener to select it.
2. Or your LinkedIn profile popped on LinkedIn Recruiter and got the Sourcer to InMail you.

Either way, you've earned the right to meet the main hiring gatekeeper: The Recruiter.

And here's where most candidates make a critical mistake: They assume the Recruiter wants to find the *best* person for the job…

Understanding the Recruiter's World

When I finally started hiring for my own team at LinkedIn, I began to see how Recruiters actually worked:

While I might have wanted to find the very best candidates, Recruiters don't have that luxury. Because unlike Hiring Managers, who are only focused on a single hire, the average Recruiter is juggling **30-40 open roles at once**.[84] And unlike the Hiring Manager, who's an expert in their space, Recruiters are expert at well… recruiting. Which means they'd be hard-pressed to definitively prove which candidate is the very best Data Scientist, Avionics Engineer, or Credit Risk Analyst.

So from both a mathematical and a practical standpoint, Recruiters don't look for the best candidate - not because they don't want to, but because they simply *can't*.

And instead, they focus on what they can do with limited time and expertise: **Find the best-*looking* candidate**. Especially since that's good for their *own* job security. After all, just like the old saying goes: "No one ever got fired for buying IBM." And so no Recruiter ever got fired for bringing in a candidate who immediately seemed awesome.

---

84   Maurer, Roy. "How Many Open Reqs Should In-House Recruiters Have?" *SHRM*, August 6, 2018. https://www.shrm.org/topics-tools/news/talent-acquisition/how-many-open-reqs-house-recruiters.

But how do they quickly find these rockstar-looking candidates? Especially with 500 resumes from the Screener, 100 LinkedIn profiles from the Sourcer, and 30-40 Hiring Managers breathing down their necks?

Simple: They use the same thing we all use when we're under pressure. **Shortcuts.**

These heuristics are so deeply baked into the Recruiter's brain because they're basically the same unconscious shortcuts humans have been taking for millennia to figure out whom to trust.

But to make them crystal clear for you, the modern job-seeker, let's bring them into the light of day...

Here's What I Did

Once I understood that Recruiters were rapidly scanning for the best-looking candidates, I realized that my new role as a job-seeker was no longer to be merely qualified - but *obviously* so. And that meant stepping-up my application game from my resume all the way into the recruiter's own company!

Step 1: I filled my resume bullets with powerful shortcuts

Even with optimized keywords, I realized my resume was still more exciting for an ATS algorithm than a human Recruiter. For example, remember these yawn-fests?

- Collaborated cross-functionally with administrators, parents, and peers to align learning objectives and drive measurable improvements

- Managed competing stakeholder priorities by building relationships with students, parents, and school leadership
- Implemented data-driven decision making by analyzing weekly assessment data to identify learning gaps and adjust instructional strategies

Technically accurate. But completely forgettable.

But then I remembered all the little biases we humans have from my undergrad Psychology course. Things like Anchoring, Loss Aversion, and Recency Bias that evolved to help us make quick decisions in times of uncertainty - and that still help guide our decision-making today.

So I drew upon three of my favorites - the Concreteness Effect, the Halo Effect, and Signaling Theory. And I translated them into resume-ese as **The 3 N's:** *Numbers, Names, and Notables.*

Finally, I rewrote every single bullet to include at least one:

1. Numbers

Our pre-frontal cortex - where we process abstract information - is the newest part of our brain, evolutionarily-speaking. Which means we're still just not as good at dealing with abstract concepts ("justice," freedom") as with concrete things ("apple," "hammer") - AKA the Concreteness Effect.[85]

---

85 Jessen, Frank, Rainer Heun, Martin Erb, D.–O. Granath, Ute Klose, Anke Papassotiropoulos, and Wolfgang Grodd. 2000. "The Concreteness Effect: Evidence for Dual Coding and Context Availability." *Brain and Language* 74 (1): 103-112. https://doi.org/10.1006/BRLN.2000.2340.

So when a Recruiter's brain reads "align learning objectives" and "drive measurable improvements," it quickly gives up and moves onto something more concrete.

On the other hand, check out this revision: "Collaborated cross-functionally to... **ensure 75% of kindergarteners read at a 1st-grade level by March.**"

The fact that the Recruiter can now imagine a classroom of tiny children reading full chapter books - that's Concreteness!

And so by using a clear and powerful Number, the bullet point not only sticks with the Recruiter longer, it also ensures the message is obvious: *This person gets results.*

2. Names

You know that annoying person at a party who can't wait to tell you they went to Harvard or work at Google? Turns out Mr. Annoying actually has a bit of evolutionary psychology working in his favor - i.e., that when someone is associated with a high-status organization or individual, some of that status rubs off on them... at least in our own eyes. That status through affiliation - that shared halo - is what psychologists call the Halo Effect.[86]

And unlike Mr. Annoying, we can put it to good use by helping the Recruiter immediately see us in that golden, heavenly light.

---

86 Thorndike, Edward L. 1920. "A Constant Error in Psychological Ratings." *Journal of Applied Psychology* 4 (1): 25–29. https://web.mit.edu/curhan/www/docs/Articles/biases/4_J_Applied_Psychology_25_(Thorndike).pdf.

For instance, let's take that humdrum bullet point: "Managed competing stakeholder priorities by building relationships with students, parents, and school leadership."

And instead of leaving the rest to the Recruiter's imagination (which, again, they don't have time to exercise on their own), we connect the dots to our very own haloes:

"Managed competing stakeholder priorities to get buy-in from parents and leadership on our new school model, **leading to coverage in *The New York Times* and *USA Today*.**"

And just like the Halo Effect, it doesn't matter if you drove the entire PR effort yourself or merely showcased your classroom to reporters, those bold-faced names signal instant credibility. So the Recruiter thinks: "If the Times trusted him, *maybe I can trust him too…*"

3. Notables

Now, I know that not every job-seeker is going to have access to big numbers and fancy names. I certainly didn't have dozens of such examples early in my career.

But it turns out that all of resume-screening - all of hiring, perhaps - boils down to a fundamental concept that every job-seeker can leverage: Signaling Theory.

This is the idea that resume-screening and hiring is all about trying to predict a really murky future based on a mere handful of signals candidates send today (essentially their application + their interview answers). And so the best way to know which signals are *real* is to focus on which signals are *expensive*.[87]

---

87 Spence, Michael. 1973. "Job Market Signaling." *The Quarterly Journal of Economics* 87 (3): 355–374. https://doi.org/10.2307/1882010.

For example, if your resume says "I'm a hard worker," that signal is completely non-credible given that it cost you nothing to claim it. On the other hand, if your resume says "I graduated with a 4.0 GPA while working my way through college full-time" - now that's a massively expensive signal (since it took a huge amount of work to accomplish) and so is massively believable (since a lazy candidate would be hard-pressed to replicate it).

And the good news is that every job-seeker has some powerful signal to send - you just need to find a useful comparison, be it your colleagues, your competition, or your context.

For instance, my school wasn't the very best school in New York City. And I definitely wasn't the very best kindergarten teacher - even in my own school. And yet, by widening the lens to our specific community, there was an expensive signal to be sent since it wasn't something that could be easily replicated.

Specifically, I started with this ho-hum bullet: "Implemented data-driven decision making by analyzing weekly assessment data to identify learning gaps and adjust instructional strategies."

And then I made it Notable: "Implemented data-driven decision making to identify learning gaps, driving our school to **outperform all other elementary schools in the neighborhood on year-end standardized tests.**"

Notice that there's no specific number or name - just a Notable signal that tells the Recruiter: "This is someone who's already moved mountains - *imagine what they could do here...*"

Step 2: I wrote a cover letter that actually mattered

While a great resume can be made to appeal to the Recruiter's need for shortcuts, even the best resume is ultimately a series of facts. And as we learned in the Sourcer section, our human brains just don't remember facts the way that we remember stories.

So what's your one chance to tell a compelling story to the Recruiter?

That's right: **Your cover letter.**

Now, I know what you're thinking: "Jeremy, no one even reads cover letters. Why not just have ChatGPT bang it out and be done with it?"

And I get it: There was a time when the majority of Recruiters said that cover letters just didn't matter.[88] Which made sense when they had other signals they could count on with a high degree of confidence.

But that time has now passed. Because we're now living in an age where almost anything can be faked - from your resume all the way to your interview (more on that in the next section).

And so the cover letter is the one chance a Recruiter has to see who you really are... **if you let them.**

Because think about that ChatGPT-generated cover letter:

"Dear Hiring Manager, I am writing to express my enthusiastic interest in X role at Y company..."

---

88   Saunders, Tracy. "Are Cover Letters Dead? We Surveyed Over 10K Recruiters and Here's What They Said." Ellevate Network, August 29, 2018. Accessed November 19, 2025. https://www.ellevatenetwork.com/articles/9422-are-cover-letters-dead-we-surveyed-over-10k-recruiters-and-here-s-what-they-said.

Even though you thought you were saving yourself time, you were really saving the Recruiter time. Because here are the three instant mental shortcuts their mind takes upon seeing that opening:

1. You clearly used AI in a lazy way.
2. You are most likely lazy yourself.
3. Lazy = Reject.

So if 89% of recruiters now expect you to write a cover letter and AI writing isn't good enough, should you go back to spending hours drafting the absolute perfect letter?[89]

No way.

Just like we discussed in Chapter 5, the Pareto Principle applies to cover letters just as much as it does to AI itself. Which means you need to write **a Pareto Cover Letter** - i.e., a letter that nails 80% of the things Recruiters actually care about with 20% of the effort.

And because Recruiters need shortcuts to find those amazing looking needles in their digital haystack, here are the three that matter most:

1. **Primacy Effect:** Does your cover letter have a *killer* opening hook? 41% of employers say this is the most important part of the letter - especially since we all

---

89 Roma Kończak, "Cover Letter Expectations for 2025—Stated by Recruiters," *Zety*, updated September 15, 2025, https://zety.com/blog/cover-letter-expectations.

tend to remember our first impressions more than our second, third, and fourth![90]

2. **Linguistic Mirroring:** Does your cover letter match the *exact* language the Recruiter listed in the job description? Research shows that matching the employer's verbiage increases your chances of a match by 23% - which isn't surprising, given the human preference for hearing our own language served back to us.[91]

3. **Affinity Bias:** Does your cover letter prove why you belong at this *specific* company - not just a generic one? 48% of HR staff admit that they're biased towards finding people who fit their company culture - which, of course, is no surprise given the tribal nature of our trust discussed in Chapter 6.[92]

Here's what that looks like in a cover letter I wrote to land my job at LinkedIn.

Opening (Primacy Effect):
"The moment I saw LinkedIn was building out a new team to help students, I knew I needed to apply. Because as someone who's spent his entire career helping others succeed in theirs, there's nothing more important to me

90 Resume Genius, "50+ Cover Letter Statistics for 2025 (Hiring Manager Survey)," 2025, https://resumegenius.com/blog/cover-letter-help/cover-letter-statistics.

91 Resumly. 2023. "Crafting Targeted Cover Letters That Mirror Job Description Language for Better Matching." Resumly Blog. https://www.resumly.ai/blog/crafting-targeted-cover-letters-that-mirror-job-description-language-for-better-matching.

92 HR News. 2017. "Less Than a Third of HR Managers Are Unprejudiced When Hiring." HR News, January 20. https://hrnews.co.uk/less-third-hr-managers-unprejudiced-hiring/.

than busting open the doors of opportunity for the next generation."

Body (Linguistic Mirroring):
"In particular, I saw that you needed someone who could help build a new team from scratch - and drive massive results in a short amount of time. And that's exactly what I did at iMentor. In the span of just 18 months, we spun up an entire online mentoring platform that was used by over 100,000 participants - from high school students in the South Bronx to female entrepreneurs in Rwanda through Goldman Sachs' 10,000 Women program."

Closing (Affinity Bias):
"But it's not just a passion for education and technology that drives me - it's a desire to be part of a team that has a clear North Star that's bigger than just the company or its products. While there are lots of great firms in Silicon Valley doing cutting-edge work, I know of very few that are harnessing technology to actually transform lives. And because I share that North Star, that obsession with real-world impact, I can think of no better place to build something meaningful."

Notice how different this is than your typical cover letter:

- Instead of losing them in the first line ("I'm writing to express my interest... blah, blah, blah") - I won the Recruiter's attention from the very first impression

- Instead of just rehashing my whole resume, I connected it directly to the Recruiter's own language and needs in a way that's not possible on a resume
- Instead of just copying-and-pasting a generic cover letter that would work for any company, I showed the Recruiter that I belonged at *this specific company*

Best of all, because I wasn't wasting time on the fluff that didn't matter - finding the company's address, writing 1,000 words that no one wanted to read - I could get the whole letter done in 10 minutes, not 10 hours.

That's the power of Pareto - both as a shortcut for you and for the Recruiter!

Step 3: I earned referrals that earned the Recruiter's trust

As effective as a powerful resume and cover letter can be for winning over the Recruiter, there's one shortcut that matters more than anything else: **Referrals.**

As discussed in Chapter 6, referrals operate at a deeper trust level than anything else in our AI-saturated world since it's just so much harder to fake relationships than any other component of your application (remember Signaling Theory?).

And the best part is that, if you applied the techniques in Chapter 6, you won't have to start from scratch with building relationships since you'll have already planted the seeds to grow your tribe.

In my case, when I was breaking into tech, I didn't necessarily have lots of deep friendships inside tech companies - but I did have initial contacts that I had found through my existing networks: classmates, fellow teachers, etc.

And so when it came time to apply to Apple, Google, and LinkedIn, I made sure to reach out to those contacts inside the companies I was excited about - and to apply all the techniques covered in the last chapter.

But this time, instead of just asking for general advice, I took everything I had learned about relationships, empathy, and generativity - and came ready with the ultimate question for the very end of these conversations:

"If you were back in my shoes as a teacher/student, knowing what you know now, what would you be doing now to get your best shot at an interview?"

Notice how this approach hits upon everything that matters:

1. **Empathy:** They really were back in your shoes once upon a time, so this immediately switches the frame from "Here's what I tell everyone" to "Here's what *I* actually did."

- **Generativity:** The essence of generativity is that you don't just want to share generic advice, you want to share your hard-won secrets - i.e., "knowing what you know now."

- **Importance:** Instead of just asking for high-level advice that doesn't really matter, this raises the stakes - i.e., getting an interview is the difference between an amazing career and one that never takes off

And because I wasn't just asking transactionally - "Hey, can you give me a referral since I'm a fellow Wolverine" - this approach led to dramatically better results. As a result, my contacts all pretty much gave the same response:

"Look Jeremy. I'll be honest - there's really only one way people get hired here: Referrals. I got referred, my whole team got referred, this whole company got referred. That's your golden ticket."

And then, after a strategic moment of silence on my part, they'd often follow-up with either:

- "So how about this? I know we're hiring right now so why don't you send me your resume and I can put in a good word for you. Who knows? Maybe I'll even get a little referral bonus."

OR

- "So here's the deal: We're not really hiring right now. But why don't you stay in touch? If we start hiring again, maybe I can refer you down the road. Cool?"

Cool? You better believe it. And you better believe that, in the latter case, I used FollowUpThen to stay in touch and got that referral when the time was right.

Because when I got that referral, it wasn't just a major shortcut for me - it was the single best shortcut for the Recruiter. Instead of crossing their fingers and hoping that a random applicant would make them look good, they now had that amazing-looking - *and trusted* - candidate they could count on.

Here's What You Should Do Now

OK, ready to become the best-looking candidate in every Recruiter's pool?

Let's go!

Step 1: Apply the 3 N's to every resume bullet

I know Resume Revisions sit somewhere below Root Canal on your list of desired activities so let's have AI get us started with this prompt:

 **PROMPT**

Scan every bullet point in my resume for the following factors:

- Does it include a Number (quantified result)?
- Does it include a Name (recognized person or organization)?
- Does it include a Notable (first, only, biggest)?

If a bullet matches none of the above, please suggest three potential revisions - one with a Number, one with a Name, and one with a Notable.

Do your best to suggest revisions that match my existing experience and avoid hallucinations.

My resume is below and my desired target audience is [Industry] Recruiters: [insert resume]

AI OUTPUT

1. "Collaborated cross-functionally with administrators, parents, and peers to align learning objectives and drive measurable improvements"

Contains:

- **Name?** No (no specific organization, so no)
- **Number?** No
- **Notable?** No ("first," "only," "record," etc.)

× **Needs revisions**
Here are **three tailored options**:

→ Add a Number

- Collaborated with administrators, parents, and peers to align learning objectives, contributing to a *15-20% improvement in student mastery scores.*

→ Add a Name

- Collaborated with school administrators, parents, and teaching teams at *[your actual school name, if you want to include it—placeholder: "Roosevelt Middle School"]* to align learning objectives and improve classroom outcomes.

> → Add a Notable
> - Collaborated with administrators, parents, and peers to create the school's *first fully aligned learning objectives framework*, resulting in measurable student progress.

Great resume bullets aren't just born - they're designed. Make sure to think about each one in the eyes of your audience!

But here's where your human skills come in - because AI is a great brainstormer but not a great empath. Which means that the above bullets all need your human intervention:

1. **Numbers:** It's true that I grew students' mastery scores - just not by 15-20%. So make sure that you leverage the inspiration but correct the specific figure.

2. **Names:** No tech Recruiter would have ever heard of my school's name - so there's a glaring lack of EQ about our audience. Instead, replace it with something that any Recruiter - or any human really - would be familiar with (e.g., "NYC Department of Education" or "Gates Foundation").

3. **Notable:** While a "fully aligned learning objectives framework" might have been a big deal for our school - it wouldn't be for a Recruiter who needs to know why you're obviously awesome. So skip the inside baseball talk and give them accomplishments that are truly notable!

Step 2: Write a Pareto Cover Letter

Because AI writing is now a Scarlet Letter for Recruiters, avoid the temptation to try to force AI to write a good one. Even if you feed it my example letter, you'll end up spending more time fighting with it ("No! I'm not a teacher like Jeremy - don't just copy his letter you idiot!!!") than if you just buckled down and wrote it yourself.

Especially since, even if you're the world's worst writer, you've got two major advantages:

1. Remember that this is a Pareto Cover Letter. Not 13 paragraphs of nonsense - but 3 paragraphs that actually matter.
2. And remember that while AI may be a terrible writer, it's an awesome researcher and connector.

So rather than face Writer's Block, start with this prompt:

 **PROMPT**

Review the below job description and my resume to identify the following:

1. What are 3 meaningful connections I have to this job that would make for a killer hook to open my cover letter?

2. For each of the bullet points in the job description, what's the bullet point from my resume that best speaks to solving this pain point?

3. Research the company's culture and identify the 3 most unique things about it (i.e., not true of every company in the industry) - and then suggest something from my resume that makes me a match with each unique cultural element.

[insert job description and Resume]

 AI OUTPUT

2) Mapping job description bullets to your resume bullets

Here's a breakdown of each bullet from the role description, and which line(s) from your resume best speak to that responsibility:

JOB DESCRIPTION BULLET	YOUR RESUME LINE(S) THAT ALIGN
Develop positioning, messaging, and narratives that clearly articulate the value of LinkedIn's Education products to learners, educators, and institutional partners.	iMentor: "led new edtech app … clients included The Gates Foundation and Goldman Sachs." – implies you positioned the product to high-level institutional partners. TFA: "generated 30% of all … applications … as a single marketer" – shows you crafted messaging that resonated broadly.

JOB DESCRIPTION BULLET	YOUR RESUME LINE(S) THAT ALIGN
Lead go-to-market planning for new features, including segmentation, launch strategy, channel recommendations, and success metrics.	iMentor: launching an edtech app, $1M revenue in two years — suggests you executed a launch and measurement strategy.
Partner with Product and Research to translate user insights into product strategy and prioritization.	Excellence Charter School: "analyzed test scores to pinpoint weaknesses and drive instruction" — shows insight → action. You also had cross-functional roles (e.g., partnership + marketing) at iMentor.

Hiring is basically just a weeks-long matching process. Help it along by showcasing that match up-front!

In addition, AI can be a great editor - especially if you help it focus on what matters. So once you use your research to write a rough draft, feel free to feed it back in like so:

🏴 PROMPT

Review the below cover letter for the following job description based on the following criteria:

1. *Primacy Effect:* Does my cover letter have a killer opening hook? Will

Recruiters feel immediately engaged and want to read more?

2. *Linguistic Mirroring:* Does my cover letter match the exact language the Recruiter listed in the job description? And do I provide clear evidence of how I can tackle that challenge?

3. *Affinity Bias:* Does my cover letter prove why I belong at this specific company - not just a generic one? Is there a clear connection between the company's values and my own?

For each of these points, please tell me what's working, what's not, and suggest the single most important thing I can do to improve.

[insert cover letter and job description]

 **AI OUTPUT**

3. Affinity Bias — Does it show why you belong at LinkedIn specifically?

What's Working

- You talk about technology trans-forming lives — a close match to LinkedIn's mission to "create economic opportunity for every member of the global workforce."

- Your career-long focus on education and opportunity aligns strongly with the Education team's purpose.

- Your tone expresses genuine mission alignment.

What's Not Working

- You reference Silicon Valley companies vaguely rather than referencing LinkedIn's actual culture.

- You are not drawing specific parallels to:

  - LinkedIn's values (Transformation, Family, Integrity, Collaboration, Results).

  - Its culture of inclusion and belonging.

  - Its data-driven approach to building the Economic Graph.

- The cover letter explains why you admire the mission, but doesn't explain why you thrive in LinkedIn's environment.

Rather than let AI write you a terrible cover letter from scratch, put it to its best use: Making your good cover letter even better!

And voila - you've got a cover letter that Recruiters will actually want to read and believe in. And it was only 50% as painful as a Root Canal - no Novocaine required!

Step 3: Earn referrals that earn the Recruiter's trust
This is the most important step - and the one most people skip because it feels uncomfortable.

But here's the good news from Chapters 3 and 6:

- You're not starting from scratch. Because you've already started to build your tribe, you've already taken the most important step - i.e., building your network *before* you need it.
- You're not asking for favors in a one-sided, transactional way. You're giving the awesome members of your tribe the ultimate gift - a chance to feel massively generative.

And here's a great shortcut to get started:

1. It turns out that you actually have a complete Company Directory for every organization in the world. No, not by hacking into their intranets but by simply searching them up on LinkedIn and clicking on their People tab:

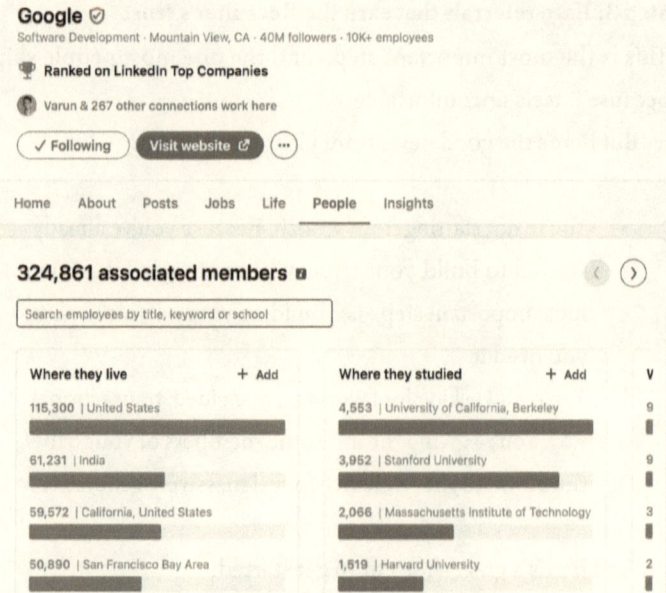

Every organization in the world has one of these People tabs... which means you have access to the company directories for every organization in the world!

2. Once you know who works there (i.e., the exact people who can refer you), start by filtering for 1st Degree Connections (people you know already) - followed by 2nd Degree Connections (friends of friends), if necessary. Just scroll to the right and set your filters accordingly!

13,423 associated members

Search employees by title, keyword or school

1st ✕   2nd ✕   Clear all

What they studied	+ Add	How you are connected
2,069	Computer Science		288,452	3rd+
1,677	Computational Science		13,158	2nd
1,456	Business Administration and Manage...		265	1st
1,364	Marketing		
1,246	Economics		

LinkedIn knows more about these employees than their employer does - which means these filters are a goldmine for finding connections!

3. If you happen to know anyone directly (e.g., someone you reached out to in Chapters 3 or 6), asking for a referral is easy because it's not just a chance for your tribemate to help you - they'll often get paid thousands of dollars (Google's average referral bonus is $5K) for spending 30 seconds uploading your resume into the ATS with their testimonial.[93]

4. But even if you only have 2nd Degree Connections, fear not - you now know exactly how to warm them

---

93 "Referral Bonus at Google," *Refer Me*, accessed November 19, 2025, https://www.refer.me/company-bonus/google.

up. Just use the power of social proof (the very same phenomenon that powers referrals themselves) and the template from Chapter 3 to ask for an intro.

5. Once you've got a conversation set-up through the warm intro, make sure you actually prepare for it. Way too many great leads go nowhere because we squander them with lame, transactional questions ("Umm... can you please refer me?"). Instead, focus on the one thing that every human loves to talk about: **Themselves.** This desire for self-disclosure runs so deep in our mental circuitry that fMRI scans show people talking about themselves activate the same part of the brain activated by food, money, and sex![94] So come ready with lots of juicy questions about *them* - not just their jobs or company - with a prompt like this:

 PROMPT

> I'd love to learn from this person. What are
> 5 juicy, open-ended questions I can ask to
> encourage them to share their experiences,
> passions, and lessons learned? Please put
> them in a logical, coherent order from
> the start to the end of the conversation.
> [attach LinkedIn profile]

94 Tamir, Diana I., and Jason P. Mitchell. "Disclosing Information about the Self Is Intrinsically Rewarding." *Proceedings of the National Academy of Sciences* 109, no. 21 (2012): 8038–8043. https://doi.org/10.1073/pnas.1202129109.

1. Early Career Inspiration

"What originally inspired you to move from teaching and education into marketing and tech, and how did that transition shape your approach to career development?"
This opens the conversation with his motivation and career pivots – from teaching and nonprofits to major tech firms like LinkedIn and Google.

2. Lessons from Big Tech

"During your time leading student marketing at LinkedIn and later at Khan Academy, what key lessons did you learn about helping people discover and grow their potential through technology?"
This draws on his high-impact roles at both organizations and invites reflections on what makes technology effective for career growth.

Think you can't be a great networker? Think again. Half of a great conversation starts with great preparation - and AI helps you focus on what really matters.

6. After building the kind of rapport that comes from asking meaningful questions, you can then pop the ultimate advice question that I used to great success. Especially since the interesting thing about giving advice to someone is that it actually makes us want to help

them *more*. Ben Franklin himself stumbled upon this phenomenon when he asked a rival legislator to lend him a book - only to discover that the legislator was now kinder to him. And the "Effect" that bears his name has now been empirically validated in dozens of studies.[95]

7. Finally, even if you don't get a referral immediately, just be sure to follow-up using the techniques from Chapter 6. I've found that if you stay in touch and show your contact how their advice has made an impact in your life, you're much more likely to get a referral than if you just have a one-off chat. As was demonstrated by the original Foot in the Door study in the 1960s, asking someone for a small favor first (e.g., put a small sticker in their window about safe driving) made them *twice* as likely to take a big action later (e.g., put up a big, ugly lawn sign with the same message).[96] So once you've got your own foot in the door, don't bail out!

AUDIENCE 4: THE HIRING MANAGER

Phew! In the gauntlet that is hiring, you've made it past the Screener, the Sourcer, and the Recruiter.

Now comes the final boss… who's literally your future boss.

---

95 Collins, Nancy L., and Lynn Carol Miller. "Self-Disclosure and Liking: A Meta-Analytic Review." *Psychological Bulletin* 116, no. 3 (1994): 457–475.

96 Freedman, Jonathan L., and Scott C. Fraser. "Compliance Without Pressure: The Foot-in-the-Door Technique." Journal of Personality and Social Psychology 4, no. 2 (1966): 195–202.

AKA the Hiring Manager - the one person who actually makes the hiring decision.

Understanding the Hiring Manager's World

I used to think of Hiring Managers as the ultimate Scantron machine. Just like the machines that graded our standardized tests back in the day, they were surely looking for right answers, the right IQ, and the right talent.

And then I became a Hiring Manager myself.

And sure, I wanted to hire rockstar professionals who could do the job.

But I also wanted to hire awesome teammates who I'd be happy to *do the job with*!

And that's when I realized that Hiring Managers aren't so robotic after all. Instead, like every human in the world, they're looking for two things in great colleagues:

1. **Competence** - Do you have what it takes to do the job well?
2. **Warmth** - Do I actually want to work with you?

Indeed, this duality has been replicated around the world - people everywhere really do want it all![97]

---

97   Susan T. Fiske, Amy J. C. Cuddy, Peter Glick, and Jun Xu, "A Model of (Often Mixed) Stereotype Content: Competence and Warmth Respectively Follow from Perceived Status and Competition," *Journal of Personality and Social Psychology* 82, no. 6 (2002): 878.

Which makes the Hiring Manager's approach to interviews so much more understandable. Because when they ask you to "Describe a time when you worked with a difficult teammate" or even "What kind of fruit are you most like," they don't actually care about the teammate or the fruit - they care about who *you* really are. And, most importantly, what you'll be like in the future!

To truly empathize with your future Hiring Manager, imagine their plight:

- They're drowning in their current workload (hence the open position)
- They're stressed about making the wrong hire (bad hires are, on average, a $17K drain on time and productivity)[98]
- They're interviewing 5-8 candidates who all look equally qualified on paper

And so every interview becomes a crystal ball to de-risk their two biggest anxieties:

1. **Competence Risk**: "What if this person can't actually deliver? What if their resume is inflated? What if I need to spend more time managing them than just doing their tasks myself?"

---

98 CareerBuilder. "75% of Employers Have Hired the Wrong Person, Here's How to Prevent That." *CareerBuilder*, accessed November 20, 2025. https://resources.careerbuilder.com/news-research/prevent-hiring-the-wrong-person.

2. **Warmth Risk**: "What if this person is toxic? What if they ruin our team's culture? What if they drive away our star performers?"

Which means that every interview is *your* chance to prove that you're more than just a "right" answer - you're the full package that puts your Hiring Manager's mind at ease.

Here's What I Did

Once I understood that Hiring Managers were desperately looking for someone they could trust on these two dimensions, I completely changed my strategy - even before the first interview.

Step 1: I started reaching out to solve Hiring Manager pain

Early on in my career, I did the same thing every proactive job-seeker does: I reached out to Recruiters.

After all, why sit on the sidelines getting rejection after rejection when you could go straight to the gatekeeper and boost your odds?

There was only one problem with this strategy: Recruiters *aren't* incentivized to respond.

As discussed in the last section, Recruiters aren't focused on hiring for a single role - but 30 or 40!

Which means they're more like **mercenaries**. While they might wish the best for every person they help hire, by the time you're hired, they're already moving on to the other 39 roles that need to be filled. And so if they stopped to do informational interviews with 10 candidates for each of those roles, they'd never get their actual job done.

No wonder, then, that my Recruiter response rate was below 5%. And even the responses I did get read more like form letters: "Thanks so much for your interest - be sure to check our Job Board for more information!"

And that's when I realized there was one neglected audience who actually did want to hear from me: **Hiring Managers**.

Because unlike Recruiters who don't bear the consequences of a bad hire (since they've long since moved on to focus on other roles), Hiring Managers bear the full brunt - probation plans, layoffs, rehiring, retraining, etc. Which I discovered through a simple LinkedIn search:

"I'm hiring."

That's it. Those two little words in the LinkedIn search box led to a torrent of posts that were basically like cries for help from inside the building:

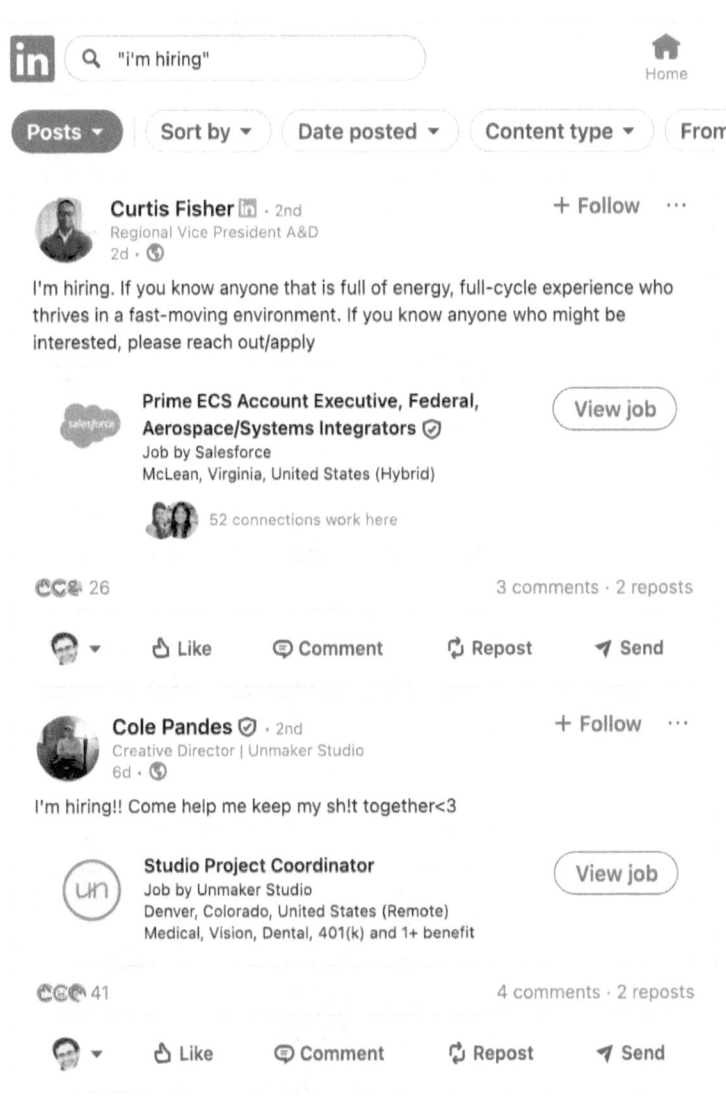

Voila, the Holy Grail of Job Searching: Your future boss revealed, before you even apply.

Which told me two things:

1. Hiring Managers *want* to hear from candidates. After all, why would they post publicly when they could just lurk in the shadows and let Recruiters be the face of the company?

2. Hiring Managers *need* to hear from awesome candidates. Behind every post on LinkedIn was a massive pain point (too much to get done, too little time) that they feel much more deeply than the Recruiter does.

So if Hiring Managers had a raging headache, I resolved to be their Advil - the candidate who tackled their challenges head-on with clear solutions.

That meant reaching out directly - but not in the ways we've discussed so far. Because a Hiring Manager isn't a friend or a tribemate. And when they've got a killer migraine, they're not in the mood for generativity.

Instead, I cut to the chase with messages like this:

I was thrilled to come across your Education Program Manager role because, as a former teacher and tech educator, I believe I can help with the exact challenges you're facing.

In particular, I noticed that you're looking to build the world's #1 EdTech Community for teachers. And having built one of the very first teacher blogs back in 2005, as well as having recruited thousands of teachers to Teach For

America's largest cohort ever, I've got a good idea about how to tackle it.

Specifically, one of the things that allowed my TFA recruiting to blow up was that I created viral cycles where prospective teachers were incentivized to share with their friends, who in turn shared with their classmates as well. And so I'm confident that we could apply a similar viral model with your community!

Notice that this message not only avoided all the general talk of tribal outreach ("I'd love to learn from you!"), but it specifically focused on two criteria every Hiring Manager cares about most:

1. **Competence:** Instead of just asserting that I was the right person for the job and then asking for a chat, it leveraged both my track record and my expertise to paint a clear picture of how I could tackle the job on Day 1.

2. **Warmth:** Instead of focusing on my own needs ("I'm really passionate about helping kids and would love to work in an EdTech company!"), the whole thing is focused on the Hiring Manager's real struggles and, as such, treats them with empathy and respect.

So it was no surprise, then, that my response rate was 5X higher than for Recruiters. And the responses I got often led to real conversations and interview opportunities. Because unlike a Recruiter, a Hiring Manager doesn't just have the power to recommend - they've got the ultimate power: *To hire!*

And so that's the person you want to get to know best.

Step 2: I won the first 5 minutes

Once I had the Hiring Manager on the phone - either for a casual conversation or a real interview - I often would retreat to Oral Exam Mode. You know the drill: The Hiring Manager would ask a question, I'd deliver my carefully memorized answer, they'd ask another question, I'd deliver another answer.

It was mechanical. Transactional. Boring.

And I never got the job.

Then I had an interview that changed everything. I was interviewing for a Program Manager role at an education nonprofit, and the Hiring Manager asked me the standard opening question:

"So, tell me about yourself."

But instead of launching into my rehearsed 2-minute monologue about my career trajectory, I paused. Looked at her tired eyes. Noticed the stack of resumes on her desk. And thought: *What does she actually need to hear right now?*

So I said: "You know, I could walk you through my entire resume. But I'm guessing you've already read it - and you probably have five more of these today. So instead, let me tell you the one thing that's not on my resume that I think matters most for this role..."

Her eyes lit up. She leaned forward.

"I got my start teaching kindergarten in Bed-Stuy. And what I learned is that the hardest part of education isn't the curriculum or the lesson plans. It's getting 25 five-year-olds with completely different backgrounds, needs, and energy levels to actually want to learn. That's program management in its purest form - and it's exactly what you need for this role working with dozens of schools across the city."

She smiled. "Tell me more about that..."

And suddenly we weren't doing an interview. We were having a conversation.

She shared her frustrations with getting buy-in from principals. I shared war stories about getting buy-in from parents. She described her challenges with teacher retention. I explained how I'd kept volunteers engaged.

We talked for 90 minutes. Way over her scheduled 30 minutes. And I got the job.

Not because I had the best answers. But because I'd given her what she actually needed: Confidence that I understood her world and could help her solve her problems.

That interview taught me something crucial: **The *first* 5 *minutes* of an interview often pre-determine the outcome.**

Why? Because of that same phenomenon from cover letter openings: The Primacy Effect - i.e., our tendency to form impressions based on initial information and then just seek evidence to confirm those impressions.

For example, if the Hiring Manager thinks you're great in the first 5 minutes, they'll spend the rest of the interview looking for positive evidence to confirm their instinct.

But if they think you're mediocre in the first 5 minutes, watch out - they'll now spend the rest of the interview looking for rope to hang you!

And the research is super clear here: The majority of Hiring Managers *admit* to making up their minds just 5 minutes into the interview.[99] I italicized the word "admit" because, let's be honest, it's pretty embarrassing to say "I waste 25 minutes of a 30-minute interview just confirming what I already believe." So I suspect it's not just the majority of Hiring Managers - but the *vast* majority.

Either way, I knew I had to win those first few precious minutes. And so based on my experience with the nonprofit interview, I developed what I call the **PET Method** - a framework for answering "Tell me about yourself" that immediately signals both competence and warmth.

Here's the structure:

 **Passion:** Start with a powerful introduction that connects your background to their specific need.

NOT: "I graduated from college in 2003 with a degree in Political Science, then I got a job as a teacher..."

BUT: "All my life, I've been passionate about using technology to improve kids' lives..."

 **Evidence:** Give 1-2 specific, quantified examples that proves you can deliver.

---

99 CareerBuilder. "1 in 2 Employers Know About a Candidate Within First 5 Minutes." accessed November 20, 2025. https://resources.careerbuilder. com/news-research/1-in-2-employers-know-about-a-candidate-within-first-5-minutes.

NOT: "After I taught, I went to work in the non-profit sector and I've worked at three organizations over the last five years..."

BUT: "That's why, as a kindergarten teacher, I taught my kids in Bed-Stuy how to use the latest software - so they'd have the skills to access opportunities their parents couldn't. And that's why I helped iMentor launch a new SaaS mentoring platform, enabling 300K kids from the Bronx to Botswana to have a great mentor for the first time."

Tie: Explicitly connect your story to what they need right now.

NOT: "So that's my background. What questions do you have?"

BUT: "Now, I'd like nothing more than to put that passion and experience to work for a company like LinkedIn that's using technology to improve millions of lives around the world."

Unlike the standard rehash of your resume that comes across as both Incompetent (a long laundry list of random events) and Cold (no sense of passion or spark), PET nails the two things that matter most:

1. **Competence:** Because it follows the flow we've learned since childhood (Thesis → Evidence → Conclusion), it's easy to follow. And the Halo Effect tells our minds that if this person is organized in their answer, there's a good chance they'll be organized as a professional.

2. **Warmth:** This answer has all the things we crave as humans - a sense of passion (not just "I need a job!"), good storytelling, and empathy for our own needs.

Which means your interviewer can now spend the next 25 minutes looking for more evidence of Competence and Warmth to confirm what they already believe about you!

Step 3: I won over the human on the other side of the table

But to really seal the deal, I had to make sure I connected with the real human in front of me - not just The Hiring Manager.

And so I went back to the one magic key to human influence that Melinda French Gates called upon in Chapter 4: *The humble story.*

And I broke it into the two components that align with the Hiring Manager's dual criteria:

1. The structure and quality of the *Stories* would be a proxy for my *Competence*

2. The delivery and engagement of my *Storytelling* would represent my *Warmth*

To develop powerhouse stories, I leaned on the same template that all great storytellers have turned to over millennia. We might call it STAR or CAR today but really, it's The Hero's Journey.

Here's how it goes:

S **Situation → Paint a Picture:** Once upon a time, there was a brand-new kindergarten teacher who was in WAY over his head...

T **Task → Hero's Challenge:** He had a class of 25 5-year olds - at the nation's first *all boys* charter school. Which means things were crazy the first day he stepped into his classroom - kids running everywhere, pure chaos.

A **Action → The Journey:** So he got to know his kids and discovered, not surprisingly, that while they didn't love reading - they were sports-obsessed. So to help them grow their vocabulary, he brought in a basketball hoop... which they were only allowed to dunk on *after* they nailed a hard word like "suspicious" or "hypothesis." And he even brought in the Assistant Athletic Director from UVA to give the kids swag - if they answered questions, of course!

R **Result → The Happy Ending:** The result was that by the end of the year, the kids didn't just like reading a little more, they were actually on their way to becoming reading superstars - with 75% reading at a first-grade level.

So as you can see, I didn't worry about which specific framework I was using. I just made sure that each story was full of juicy details (brand-new teacher, all-boys school), big challenges (classroom chaos!), and satisfying resolutions (reading conquers all).

Because if I could transform the random experience of teaching kindergarten into a powerful story, there's a good chance I could be a highly competent colleague.

And then, to bring the stories to life, I began to sharpen my storytelling craft. That meant diving into the key aspects of connection:

- **Vocal Tone + Gestures:** Research shows that listeners strongly prefer speech with dynamic tones (changing from high to low or vice-versa) and gestures.[100] They're so important to interviews that MIT researchers built a model that could predict interview outcomes with an 85% success rate based on tone and gestures alone![101]

- **Length of Speech:** While an interview might seem like an invitation to give a long monologue on your experience, avoid the temptation! Research consistently shows that giving your interviewer a chance to have a back-and-forth *dialogue* leads to significantly improved perceptions.[102]

---

100 Rodero, Emma, et al. "Effectiveness, Attractiveness, and Emotional Response to Voice Pitch and Hand Gestures in Public Speaking." *Frontiers in Communication* (2022). https://www.frontiersin.org/articles/10.3389/fcomm.2022.869084/full.

101 Soman, Vikrant, and Anmol Madan. "Social Signaling: Predicting the Outcome of Job Interviews from Vocal Tone and Prosody." MIT Media Lab, March 2009. https://vismod.media.mit.edu/tech-reports/TR-637.pdf.

102 Khalil, Alexander, Gabriella Musacchia, and John Rehner Iversen. "It Takes Two: Interpersonal Neural Synchrony Is Increased after Musical Interaction." *Brain Sciences* 12, no. 3 (2022): 409. https://doi.org/10.3390/brainsci12030409.

- **Vulnerability:** It might feel safer to hold back your true emotions in such a high-stakes scenario. And yet, there's ample research that shows that by disclosing your authentic feelings - even mistakes you've made - you actually come across as more likable and trustworthy.[103]

Because here's the real deal: No Hiring Manager hires a resume or a LinkedIn profile. They hire a living, breathing person - warts and all. And if we're going to spend more time with this person than our own friends and family, that better be time well-spent. So by investing in a little Warmth and Storytelling magic in your interview, you can give them the confidence that those next many hours, days, and years will be just that!

Here's What You Should Do Now

Ready to win over Hiring Managers and land offers? Here's your step-by-step playbook.

Step 1: Reach out to solve Hiring Manager pain

Why wait to meet the Hiring Manager until you have an interview? Especially since they're calling out for your talent today. Here's how to find them and respond:

---

103 Collins, Nancy L., and Lynn C. Miller. "Self-Disclosure and Liking: A Meta-Analytic Review." *Psychological Bulletin* 116, no. 3 (1994): 457-475. https://labs.psych.ucsb.edu/collins/nancy/UCSB_Close_Relationships_Lab/Publications_files/Collins%20and%20Miller%2C%201994.pdf.

1. Search LinkedIn posts for the phrase "I'm hiring" along with your desired job title. Then filter by "Past week" since research shows that you're 8X more likely to earn an interview if you apply in the first few days than if you apply after the first week.[104]

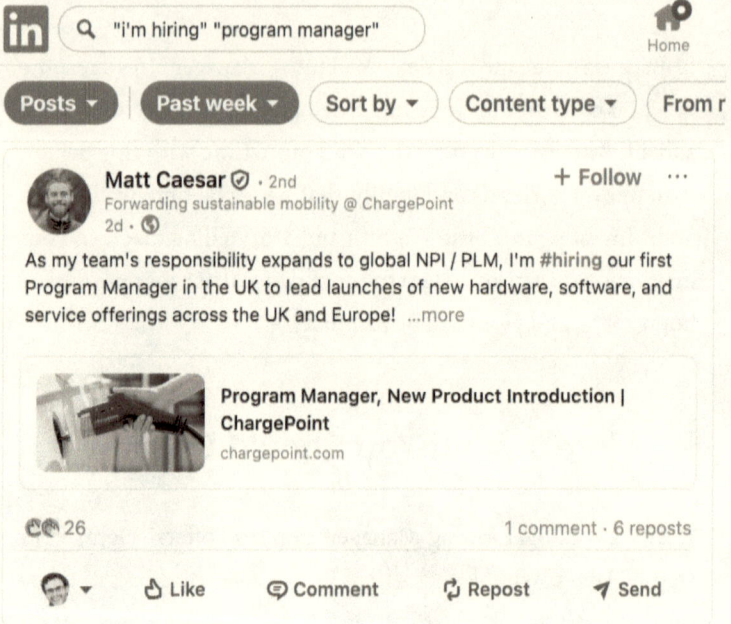

Notice that these aren't recruiters or headhunters - instead, they're your future boss!

2. Once you find a specific job you're excited about, run the job description through AI with a similar prompt to the one we used for our Pareto Cover Letter research:

---

104 Russi, Erika. "The Data Behind the Job Search: When to Apply." *Medium*, January 21, 2019. https://medium.com/@erika.russi/the-data-behind-the-job-search-39065bb3cdd7.

PROMPT

What are the 3 biggest pain points the hiring manager is trying to solve with the below job opening? For each pain point, suggest a specific experience from my resume that proves I can provide a powerful solution.

[insert job description + Resume]

AI OUTPUT

1. Pain Point: Coordinating complex, cross-functional hardware launches without delays

What the role requires:
ChargePoint's NPI PM is expected to orchestrate engineering, supply chain, manufacturing, quality, and operations teams so new charging hardware ships on time, passes testing milestones, and smoothly transitions to mass production. This is a coordination-heavy role with high visibility and high risk if timelines slip.

How your background solves this pain point:

☑ **iMentor – Led a new edtech app to $1M in revenue within two years**
This demonstrates:

- Running a multi-stakeholder initiative from concept to scaled launch

- Managing technical teams + users + executives with competing needs

- Delivering a product on a deadline
  and hitting real business outcomes

Your experience launching a new product and
driving it to meaningful adoption is exactly
the real-world execution proof they want.

*No one hires just for the fun of it. Understand the Hiring
Manager's pain and you're halfway to getting hired!*

3. If the Hiring Manager is a 2nd Degree Connection, you
   can ask for an introduction from your mutual contact
   (and, of course, ask them to vouch for you if they know
   your work well). But if not, here's a prompt to track down
   their email address (since you can safely assume they'll
   be checking that more often than their LinkedIn inbox):

 PROMPT

What is the most common email format for
employees at [company]?

Example:

 PROMPT

What is the most common email format for
employees at ChargePoint?

 **AI OUTPUT**

> The most common email format at Charge-Point, Inc. appears to be:
> first.last@chargepoint.com – used by roughly 92–95% of addresses.

Don't waste a cent on those overpriced email lookup tools. Thanks to AI, you can crack the code on any employee email in seconds... for $0.

4. With your research completed, you can now reach out using a template similar to my own outreach:

 Subject: Tackling the [biggest challenge]

I was thrilled to come across your [job title] role because, as a [most relevant background], I believe I can help with the exact challenges you're facing.

In particular, I noticed that you're [biggest pain point]. And having [most relevant accomplishment], I've got a good idea about how to tackle it.

Specifically, [your plan for tackling it].

You can see more on my LinkedIn profile: [link]. But if you have 10 minutes to chat next week, I'd love to learn more about [challenge] and share some of the techniques that have - and haven't - worked in my experience.

Sincerely,
[your name]

Step 2: Win the first 5 minutes

Once you've begun your outreach, it's time to start winning the first 5 minutes of your conversations - which, as mentioned, often leads to winning the job, too.

Use this prompt to get started:

PROMPT

> Based on my resume and this job description, help me craft an answer for "Tell me about yourself" using this framework:
>
> 1. PASSION: Suggest 3 unique parts of my background that make me the perfect fit for this role
>
> 2. EVIDENCE: For each of those unique points of passion, recommend a specific experience that best demonstrates that passion in action
>
> 3. TIE: For each passion point, suggest a natural connection that ties that characteristic back to what the Hiring Manager needs to accomplish with this role
>
> [insert resume and job description]

🤖 AI OUTPUT

PASSION 1 — I love building order, clarity, and results out of complex, cross-functional work.

EVIDENCE
At **Echoing Green**, you recruited and coordinated **300+ senior executives** to evaluate business plans, managing a multi-stage process that produced **2,000+ hours of structured review**. You kept dozens of moving parts aligned, ensuring consistency, quality, and on-time decisions.

TIE to ChargePoint NPI
New Product Introduction is all about orchestrating engineering, supply chain, manufacturing, quality, and operations. Your ability to coordinate large, diverse groups and drive predictable outcomes maps directly to **keeping NPI builds on schedule**, managing program gates, and ensuring cross-functional teams stay aligned through **design → pilot → production**.

Don't waste the Hiring Manager's time by reciting your resume from memory. Instead, give them just what matters most - and nothing more.

From the options that AI suggests, pick the path that feels most natural to you - and then put it in your own words. Because, as mentioned, the Hiring Manager isn't looking to hire a robotic ghostwriter - they want someone who can bring those words to life in-person.

Step 3: Win over the human on the other side of the table

To truly bring those words to life, you're going to need to practice your delivery. But not just in front of a mirror. Because research on the world's top performers - athletes, musicians, and even chess grandmasters - shows that the most effective practice requires immediate, specific feedback.[105] Otherwise, you're just reinforcing bad habits.

So if you've got your own career coach, great! But if not, here's a complete guide to turning AI into your feedback-focused coach:

1. Start by getting your stories ready. There's no point in practicing delivery if you don't have amazing, high Competence stories ready to deliver. So to focus your story creation, go back to the Hiring Manager's pain points and convert them into interview questions like so:

PROMPT

```
What are the primary pain points behind this
job description? And for each pain point,
what is the most likely interview question?

[insert job description]
```

---

105 Macnamara, Brooke N., David Z. Hambrick, and Frederick Oswald. "Deliberate Practice and Performance in Music, Games, Sports, Education, and Professions: A Meta-Analysis." *Psychological Science* 25, no. 8 (2014): 1608–18.

AI OUTPUT

1. Pain Point: Ensuring on-time delivery of new hardware/software products across cross-functional teams

What the job requires:
The role emphasizes program schedules, product readiness activities, identifying and mitigating risks proactively, and owning end-to-end program execution.

Likely interview questions:

- "Tell me about a time when you managed a product launch that was at risk of missing its deadline. What did you do to get it back on track?"

- "How have you coordinated engineering, manufacturing, supply chain, and operations to deliver a product on time — describe the schedule you used, the key milestones, and how you handled delays."

How do Hiring Managers decide what to ask you about? It's not a guessing game - they start with their pain and work towards solutions. So should you!

2. Next, shape your stories to match those questions, drawing upon a proven framework:

PROMPT

Generate STAR stories for each of those questions based on my resume. Make sure that the answers come across as both Competent and Warm.

[insert resume]

AI OUTPUT

☆ 1. "Tell me about a time you managed a product launch that was at risk of missing its deadline."

(Based on your iMentor product-launch experience)

S – Situation
When I was at iMentor, we were developing a new edtech platform for major partners like the Gates Foundation. Midway through the build, shifting requirements and unclear engineering milestones put the launch date at real risk — and teams were losing confidence.

T – Task
I needed to stabilize the project, realign stakeholders, and rebuild a realistic,

cross-functional path to launch without compromising product quality.

A – Action
I brought together engineering, product, and client-facing teams for a single planning session where we mapped every dependency and clarified responsibilities. I created a unified schedule with clear decision points, introduced structured weekly checkpoints, and implemented rapid user-testing loops so engineers could course-correct quickly.

R – Result
We regained momentum, launched on time, and the platform went on to generate **over $1M in revenue in two years**. More importantly, the team felt supported and aligned – we turned a stressful situation into a collaborative win.

STAR isn't just a human storytelling recipe - it's a formula that helps AI translate our random experiences into interview gold.

3. Finally, head over to an AI-powered interview practice tool like Yoodli. Here, you can upload the desired job description and it will generate a custom mock interview.

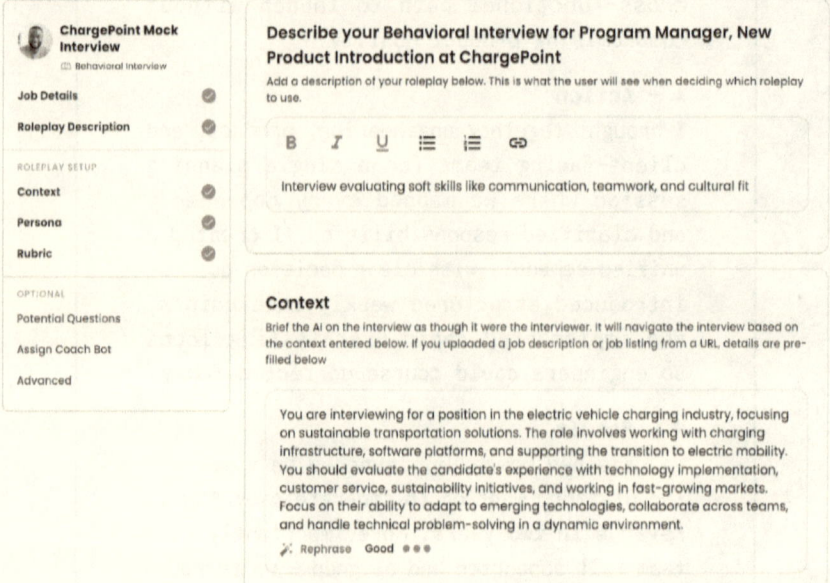

*Want to accelerate your interview skill development? Don't
just practice for generic interviews - get specific ASAP.*

4. But the key is to not just go through the motions,
but to actually push yourself to *improve* based on the
feedback you get at the end. For example, can you use
the feedback you receive on your STAR answers to
improve your perceived Competence by telling more
detailed, coherent stories in your next session? And
can you take the feedback you get on Tone, Gestures,
and Length of Speech to ensure that you're coming
across as Warm as possible? That's what the world's best
performers do - and now that's what you can do, too!

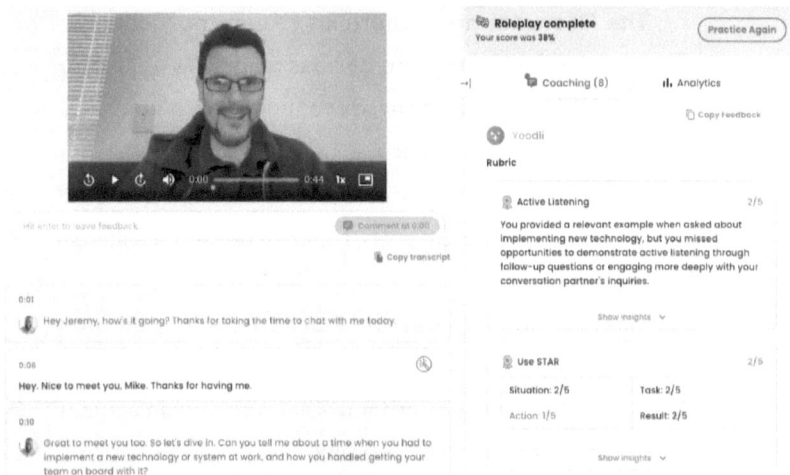

Yoodli is like the career coach we all need - but can't always afford. It tells you exactly what you need to improve - and then comes back for Round 2 right away!

THE BOTTOM LINE: EMPATHY IS YOUR SUPERPOWER

Let's zoom back out for a second.

You've now learned how to win over four completely different audiences:

- **The Screener** needs obvious qualification signals they can identify in 12 seconds
- **The Sourcer** needs LinkedIn profiles optimized for both algorithms and human eyes

- **The Recruiter** needs shortcuts (Numbers, Names, Notables) to identify safe, obvious candidates
- **The Hiring Manager** needs confidence that you're both competent and warm

Each audience has different goals. Different pressures. Different decision-making processes.

And the candidates who win? They aren't necessarily the most qualified on paper.

They're the ones who understand what each person actually needs - and give it to them authentically.

That's empathy.

And in the Age of AI, where technical perfection is becoming commoditized, empathy is your unfair advantage.

BUT LANDING THE JOB IS JUST THE BEGINNING

Here's what most career advice gets wrong: It treats getting hired like crossing a finish line.

You optimized your resume. You aced the interviews. Mission accomplished, right?

Wrong.

Getting the job is actually the start of an entirely new race.

Because while everyone else is celebrating their offer letter and coasting into their first week, the professionals who truly thrive are already thinking three moves ahead. They're asking: *How do I become so valuable that this company would never let me go?*

That's what separates people who get laid off in the next downturn from people who not only survive, but even get promoted.

And in the AI age, where companies can automate more technical work than ever, the question isn't just "Can *you* do the job?"

It's: "Do I want to do the job *with you*?"

That's exactly what Chapter 8 is about.

Not just showing up and doing your tasks. But becoming the colleague that AI can never replace - the one who brings energy instead of draining it, focuses on what matters instead of wasting time, and takes ownership instead of waiting to be told.

The one who makes their manager think: *"This person is absolutely essential to everything we're trying to do."*

Ready to become unbreakable in your role?

Let's go.

8

HOW TO SUCCEED IN YOUR NEXT JOB

t's my first month at LinkedIn, and I'm sitting in a product meeting feeling like I've made a terrible mistake.

I'm the new marketer on the Education Team. Fresh from teaching kindergarten and working at nonprofits. Eager to prove myself in Silicon Valley.

And the Product Leader - let's call her Miranda - is staring at me like I'm a waste of oxygen.

"What are you even doing here?" she says, not quietly. "You can't code. You can't design. You can't do data science. Come back when you can do something useful."

The room goes silent. Everyone's looking at their laptops.

And I'm thinking: *She's right. What AM I doing here?*

Because here's what I knew about myself: I wasn't the natural tech genius who could spin up a prototype in an afternoon. I wasn't the charismatic extrovert who could charm everyone in the room. I wasn't even the person with a fancy degree from Stanford to wear as my suit of armor.

I was a former kindergarten teacher who liked helping people and had somehow convinced LinkedIn to take a chance on me.

And in that moment, I realized: I couldn't just show up and coast on talent or pedigree. I had to become the teammate that everyone *wanted* to work with - the person who made Miranda's life easier, not harder.

So that's exactly what I did.

I started going out into the field, talking to students and career coaches about what they actually needed. I brought back real insights, not just opinions. When Miranda had a problem, I came with three solutions and a recommendation. When she needed data, I didn't just dump a spreadsheet on her - I curated it down to the insights that mattered.

I became obsessed with making myself useful.

Six months later, Miranda pulled me aside. "You know what? You're actually a pretty handy teammate after all... at least for a marketer."

Which, in a crazy competitive world like Silicon Valley, is practically like winning the MVP trophy!

And here's the crazier thing: Everything I learned about becoming a great teammate over a decade ago is doubly true today. That's because, as discussed throughout this book, the skills that Miranda craved in 2012 - coding, design, data science - are now becoming commoditized. Whereas, the very things that make us a great teammate - the things that make us human in the first place - are now more valuable than ever.

THE ULTIMATE AI-PROOF CAREER INSURANCE

Here's what most people miss about AI disruption: They think the threat is that AI will replace their technical skills.

But that's only the 1st Order Effect.

What happens after AI is better at technical work than most humans?

Now we get to the 2nd Order Effect: Who does the boss still want on their team when they no longer have to put up with technically gifted jerks?

Think about it: If AI can do 80% of your technical work, the only reason to keep you around is if you make work *better* for everyone else. If you're the person who:

- Makes meetings productive instead of painful
- Communicates clearly instead of confusingly
- Delivers results instead of excuses
- Brings energy instead of drama
- Solves problems instead of creating them

Then you're not competing with AI. You're providing the exact value AI *can't* replicate.

Research has backed this up for over a century. For example, back in 1918, the Carnegie Foundation interviewed engineers - the very people who depended on technical skills for their livelihoods - and 85% of them said that personal qualities (integrity, resourcefulness, initiative, tact, etc.) were more important to engineering success than technical knowledge.[106]

Why? Because even during the Industrial Age, organizations were desperate for people who made work *easier* for everyone around them. And in the AI Age, that desperation is only intensifying.

THE ACE FRAMEWORK: BECOMING IRREPLACEABLE

After studying what made people successful across Silicon Valley, entrepreneurship, and the modern working world, in general, I've identified three core qualities that separate great teammates from mediocre ones:

A is for **Agreeableness** - Being the person who energizes others instead of draining them

C is for **Conscientiousness** - Showing respect by focusing on what matters most instead of wasting others' time

E is for **Experimentation** - Taking ownership and trying new approaches instead of just maintaining the status quo

---

106 Mann, Charles Riborg. *A Study of Engineering Education, Prepared for the Joint Committee on Engineering Education of the National Engineering Societies.* Bulletin No. 11. Boston: Merrymount Press for the Carnegie Foundation for the Advancement of Teaching, 1918. https://archive.org/details/studyofengineeri00mannrich.

Note that these qualities build upon each other in order, in the same way that we judge each other via first impressions - and then get to know each other more deeply over time. So Agreeableness is the *foundation* - if you don't win over your new teammates with positive energy, you won't get a chance to drive results and try new things. But if you're *only* Agreeable, you also won't achieve your full MVP teammate potential - since that only comes with being Conscientious and Experimental.

Finally, just to make these characteristics easier to visualize, I've distilled them into the **10 Commandments of Great Teammates** - i.e., the specific behaviors that will make you indispensable in the future, no matter what AI does next.

Let's break them down.

AGREEABLENESS: BRINGING ENERGY INSTEAD OF DRAINING IT

Here's What I Did

When I joined LinkedIn's Education Team, I thought I'd landed my dream job. Helping students discover career opportunities through technology? Sign me up.

But reality hit fast.

We were building products for college students at a time when students were obsessed with Facebook (which was also working on its own job search tool). In focus groups, they literally described

LinkedIn as "Facebook for old people." Not exactly the ringing endorsement we were hoping for.

And internally? We were spinning our wheels, failing to make progress on any of the features we had planned. Things got so bad at one point that our team got marched down to the corporate cafeteria to get chewed out by the VP of Product and the CTO!

Between pushback from the outside and friction within, I watched morale crater. People started burning out. The team that had been excited six months earlier now felt defeated.

And I realized: If I kept absorbing all this negativity without doing something about it, I'd burn out too. Or worse, I'd start contributing to the downward spiral.

So I did something that was totally unnatural for me: I became a **Happy Warrior.**

Even though I'm a born introvert and cynic, I realized that I needed to ditch my usual Devil's Advocate mentality if we were going to prove the doubters wrong.

Not by bringing fake positivity. Or pretending problems didn't exist. But by actively fighting to find solutions and keep the team energized when everything felt impossible.

Here's what that looked like in practice:

- **I communicated authentically.** When things weren't going well at first, I was tempted to hide behind corporate-speak. You know the drill: "Due to ongoing macro headwinds, engagement in our target demographic is below desired OKRs this quarter." And yet, I knew this obfuscation was only going to make the problem worse. So I admitted to my brand-new boss that we were failing at every key step of the process - from student perceptions all the way through in-product experience. But by being candid up-front, I earned her and the team's trust to discover solutions to those challenges instead of just hiding from them.

- **I said "Yes, and..." instead of "Yeah, but..."** One of my new boss's first suggestions was to make a video that tackled students' negative perception of the site. My natural inclination was to say: "Yeah, but that won't change any of the fundamental issues we're having with launching products." But instead, I leaned into the project - even adding the line from our focus groups: "LinkedIn isn't just for old guys with heavy briefcases" (which our CEO hated since those old guys were our biggest customers!). Then, once the video started doing well on YouTube, we got buy-in to start it running as an ad on other videos. As the views grew and grew, the CEO even asked us to screen it at the next big company-wide meeting. Within a few months, it was the most-watched video in LinkedIn's history - and proof positive that our team was on the right track.

- **I showed people they mattered.** When teammates did good work, I didn't just thank them privately. I Cc'd their bosses. I called out their contributions in meetings. I made sure leadership knew exactly who was driving our wins. But I also made it a point to have lunch with every single person on the team at least once - even people totally outside my space like WebDevs, Data Scientists, and Designers. That way, I actually knew what mattered to them and could give them recognition for the things they were genuinely proud of, not just what I assumed mattered.

The result?

After all that time wandering in the desert, we made it to the Promised Land: Students became the fastest-growing demographic on LinkedIn and the site became the #1 destination for student job-seekers - blowing Facebook and all other would-be competitors out of the water.

And as icing on the cake, I won the company's inaugural Reid Hoffman Prize - an award given to the employees who best embodied LinkedIn's core values of collaboration and customer focus.

Not because I was the smartest person on the team. Not because I had the best ideas. But because I'd figured out that in challenging times, the most valuable thing you can bring is energy that lifts others up instead of dragging them down.

Here's What You Should Do

Being agreeable isn't about being fake. It's about being that essential teammate who energizes others instead of draining them. Here are the three core commandments to become your team's Happy Warrior - even if you're a pessimist at heart:

1. Thou Shalt Communicate Like a Human, Not a Robot

As bad as corporate-speak was in 2012, it's 100X worse today. That's because AI has been trained on all that nonsense and now spouts it off on the regular. And so we frequently find ourselves on the receiving end of messages like "We are thrilled to embark on this exciting journey of collaboration and innovation." Ugh - gross!

So, before you find yourself tempted to send such a message, just remember how receiving it makes you feel - that massive ick-factor, that fundamental sense of disrespect. In fact, research shows that AI communication is so repellent that it leads to significant erosion in trust and confidence - the very elements a team needs to run effectively.[107]

So feel free to use AI to review your messages if you like, but please, please, please: Write them in your **own** voice first. Using AI to communicate with your teammates isn't a time-saver. It's a relationship-killer.

Bonus Hack: Really need AI to help you with a difficult message? Try asking AI for an outline first to avoid falling into the corporate-speak trap:

 PROMPT

> I need to communicate the following message: [idea of your message]
>
> Please generate a detailed outline of the best way to clearly and powerfully convey the message - BUT DO NOT write the message directly. Allow me to draft it in my own voice before providing feedback on its clarity and efficacy.

---

107 Cardon, Peter W., and Anthony W. Coman. "Professionalism and Trustworthiness in AI-Assisted Workplace Writing: The Benefits and Drawbacks of Writing With AI." *International Journal of Business Communication*, 2025. https://doi.org/10.1177/23294884251350599.

2. Thou Shalt Say "Yes, And…" Instead of "Yeah, But…"

When your teammates are getting worn down by problems, be the person who fights for solutions and keeps the team's energy up. Not fake positivity - real, earned optimism from actually solving problems together. When everyone else is spiraling into "this will never work," you're the one asking "okay, what if we tried it this way instead?" The teammates who bring this energy become the ones everyone wants on their projects, because they make hard work feel possible, not impossible.

> *Bonus Hack:* Are you really stumped by an idea your team-mate is pushing? Sometimes AI can actually play the role of Devil's Advocate - but against our own pessimism! Here's a prompt you can try to see the potential upside, even if it's not immediately clear to you:

 PROMPT

```
A teammate just suggested this idea: [idea
you're skeptical about]

Help me find:

1. What's valid/valuable about this idea?
2. What are the most valid concerns?
3. How could we modify the idea to keep the
value while addressing concerns?
```

3. Thou Shalt Show the Love

Make your teammates' wins visible to leadership. When someone does great work, go beyond a private "nice job." Loop in their manager on the email thread. Highlight their specific contributions during team meetings. Ensure the people with power to promote and reward them actually see what they're accomplishing. This isn't about politics - it's about making sure good work gets recognized in a world where everyone's overwhelmed and great contributions often go unnoticed.

But recognition isn't enough. You also need genuine connection. So make time to have lunch (or virtual coffee) with everyone on your team - even people outside your immediate area. Get to know where they're from, what they do, and, most importantly, what really matters to them.

Think this would be a huge pain in the butt for your colleagues? Think again.

Everyone has to eat or grab a cup of coffee, and it turns out we're all actually happier when we connect with others - *even if we're introverts*. For instance, when University of Chicago researchers asked train commuters to chat with a stranger, they thought: "Ugh, this is going to suck!" And yet, the people who had a conversation with a stranger were way more satisfied than those who sat in silence.[108]

So make time to connect. It's not a distraction from work - it's the essential foundation that makes work better.

---

108 Epley, Nicholas, and Juliana Schroeder. "Mistakenly Seeking Solitude." *Journal of Experimental Psychology: General* 143, no. 5 (2014): 1980-1999. https://doi.org/10.1037/a0037323.

Bonus Hack: Worried about how you're going to connect with someone in a totally different role? Or is small talk your kryptonite? Fear not - here's a quick prompt to come ready for a fun conversation. Just remember what we discussed earlier in the book - people love to share what they've learned and are passionate about so stick to those topics and you'll be golden:

 **PROMPT**

> I'm going to have a quick chat with this person: [insert name and company]
>
> What are 10 questions I can ask them about their passions, learnings, and goals?

CONSCIENTIOUSNESS: RESPECTING TIME INSTEAD OF WASTING IT

Here's What I Did

After my experience at LinkedIn, I thought I'd cracked the code of being a great teammate.

Be positive. Say "Yes" to everything. Schedule a lot of meetings and make everyone feel included.

I was basically the Golden Retriever of coworkers - eager, enthusiastic, and always happy to help with whatever anyone needed.

And for a while, it worked great. People liked working with me. I got invited to interesting projects. Leadership saw me as a team player.

But then two things happened in rapid succession that completely shattered my understanding of what it meant to be a good teammate.

First, I got really sick.

It was December 2021 - right in the middle of the Omicron COVID wave. I'd joined Khan Academy a few years earlier, excited to help build the future of education. And then I got hit with a mystery illness that put me on bedrest for three months.

Not COVID, ironically. But something that left me so exhausted I could barely sit up for more than 30 minutes at a time.

Lying in bed, watching my life pass me by, I started seeing my old approach from a completely different angle. All those random projects I agreed to? I wasn't being collaborative - I was just filling up my fleeting hours with busywork. All those meetings I'd scheduled? They weren't helping people - they were stealing their time.

And suddenly, the Golden Retriever approach didn't seem so great anymore. Life was just too short.

Then, when I finally recovered, Khan Academy asked me to lead the Marketing Team.

Ten people. All looking to me for direction. All with their own projects, their own meetings, their own emails flooding their inboxes.

And I realized: If I led my teammates the way I'd operated as an individual contributor, I'd be wasting their lives too.

So I made a radical shift.

- **I stopped saying "Yes" to everything and started saying "Hell yes" to one thing.** That one thing became our North Star: Launch Khanmigo, the world's first AI-powered tutor. Every project, every meeting, every email had to ladder up to that goal. If it didn't? We cut it.

- **I ruthlessly protected everyone's time.** I canceled recurring meetings that had become status update theater. When we did meet, I'd send a tight agenda beforehand: three topics, 30 minutes max, here's what we need to actually get done. People started showing up prepared because they knew I wasn't going to waste their time.

- **I put the team on a data diet.** Even though I had always been the guy who overcommunicated with his teammates (to make sure everyone had full information), I started to see the dark side of this approach with the rise of AI. All of a sudden, people were sending out research reports and project plans that were clearly AI-generated. How did I know? Because what used to be one page was now 26 pages! So, to model the change we needed, I made sure to leave the AI slop in ChatGPT and only sent out the most critical insights - i.e., the human-curated part that was valuable, not all the junk that just wasted people's time.

- **I insisted we take shots on goal.** As much as I had embraced strategy docs and endless review sessions before getting sick, I now realized that there just aren't enough working hours in a lifetime to justify the cost. So I asked our team to only prioritize "shots on goal" - i.e., real work, out there in the real world, that had a real chance of moving the needle on our North Star.

The result?

In one year, our tiny nonprofit team launched the world's first AI-powered tutor and generated over $1 million in revenue. Not because we worked more hours than anyone else. But because we were ruthlessly focused on what actually mattered - and we didn't waste anyone's time pretending otherwise.

And here's what I learned: Being agreeable - being the nice, positive teammate - that's table stakes. But being conscientious? That's how you become irreplaceable.

Here's What You Should Do

Conscientiousness isn't about working harder. It's about working in a way that respects others' time and the team's ultimate goal. Here are the four core commandments:

4. Thou Shalt Keep Your Eyes on the Prize

The single biggest mistake most people make? They confuse motion with progress.

They're in meetings. They're sending emails. They're collaborating on seventeen different initiatives. They feel busy, productive, valuable.

But when you ask "What's your #1 goal?" they give you that deer-in-headlights look.

Here's what I learned the hard way: You can't be a great teammate if you're pulling people in seventeen different directions.

Research backs this up. Studies on goal-setting show that people who focus on a single, clearly defined objective are significantly more likely to achieve it than those juggling multiple competing priorities.[109] Why? Because every additional goal doesn't just add complexity - it multiplies it. Three goals means constant tradeoff decisions. Five goals means paralysis.

So here's your first job: Pick your North Star.

Not three North Stars. Not "my top priorities." ONE goal that everything else ladders up to.

For our team at Khan Academy, it was "Launch Khanmigo." Every marketing campaign, every partnership conversation, every dollar spent had to answer one question: "Does this get us closer to making the world's first AI-powered tutor a massive success?"

If the answer was "Yes" - we did it. If the answer was "Maybe someday" - we cut it. If the answer was "Well, it's also important that we..." - we definitely cut it.

Bonus Hack: Struggling to identify your North Star? Use this prompt to cut through the noise:

🤓 PROMPT

```
I'm currently working on these projects:
[list everything on your plate]

Help me identify my North Star goal by:

1. Finding the common thread across these
projects
2. Eliminating anything that's just "keeping
the lights on"
```

---

109 Zhang, Ying, Ayelet Fishbach, and Arie W. Kruglanski. "The Dilution Model: How Additional Goals Undermine the Perceived Instrumentality of a Shared Path." *Journal of Personality and Social Psychology* 92, no. 3 (March 2007): 389–401. https://pubmed.ncbi.nlm.nih.gov/17352599.

> 3. Suggesting one overarching objective that would make everything else easier or unnecessary
>
> Format your answer as: "Your North Star is: [ONE specific, measurable goal]"

5. Thou Shalt Respect Others' Time Like It's Your Own

Let me paint you a picture of my old meeting style:

60-minute recurring weekly check-ins with everyone on the team. No agenda - we'd just give everyone a chance to share what they wanted to. I'd start with "So what are you working on?" and we'd meander through status updates, random tangents, and "while I have you here..." topics.

I thought I was being collaborative. Building relationships. Keeping everyone informed.

I was actually being a time thief.

Here's the math that hit me when I was bedridden: If I have a 60-minute meeting with 10 people, that's 10 hours of collective time. For that meeting to be worth it, I need to create MORE than 10 hours of value.

Most meetings don't come close.

Research shows the average knowledge worker now has between 8-17 meetings per week, and they rate 71% of those meetings as "failures" - meaning the meetings could have been an email, or didn't need to happen at all.[110]

---

110 ASE, "Meeting Fatigue: How Too Many Meetings Have Employees Feeling Enraged Instead of Engaged," ASEonline.org, accessed December 12, 2025, https://www.aseonline.org/News-Events/Articles/meeting-fatigue-how-too-many-meetings-have-employees-feeling-enraged-instead-of-engaged.

So to save your colleagues from this temporal black hole, here are **The 7 Deadly Sins of Meeting Gluttony:**

1. **The Sin of Unnecessary Congregation:** Look, meetings exist for exactly two purposes: tightly-bounded brainstorming or making critical decisions. That's it. If you're just sharing updates, you don't need to trap eight people in a conference room for 30 minutes. Send an email. Post in Slack. Record a quick Loom video. Save the face-to-face time for when you actually need to hash something out together or make a hard choice.

2. **The Sin of Indiscriminate Invitation.** Don't invite your whole team plus all your cross-functional partners "just to be safe." This is CYA masquerading as collaboration. You know what people actually want more than being included? *Having their time back.*

3. **The Sin of the Agenda-Less Ambush.** A meeting without an agenda isn't an awesome chance to chill with your work homies - it's a disrespectful statement that says "your time isn't valuable enough for me to get organized."

4. **The Sin of the Massive Meeting.** Here's a secret: The human attention span for focused discussion is about 20 minutes.[111] After that, people are checking their phones, thinking about lunch, or mentally drafting their grocery list. If you schedule an hour, you're essentially

---

111 Bligh, Donald A. *What's the Use of Lectures?* San Francisco: Jossey-Bass, 2000. ISBN 978-0787951628.

announcing "I plan to waste at least 30 minutes of your day." Schedule 30 minutes maximum. And if you can't cover your agenda in 30 minutes, your agenda is too ambitious for actual human brains.

5. **The Sin of the Autopilot Meeting.** Recurring meetings feel so responsible when you schedule them: "Now we'll always be aligned!" Six months later, nobody remembers why the meeting exists, but it's still eating 90 minutes of everyone's week because canceling it feels harder than just showing up. Recurring meetings are organizational plaque - they build up slowly but eventually kill your team's productivity.

6. **The Sin of the Meeting Monologue.** Don't invite people to a meeting, only to talk *at them* for 25 minutes straight. If you're going to force someone to show up, at least give them a chance to contribute. Otherwise, what you want isn't a meeting - it's an audience for your TED talk.

7. **The Sin of being afraid to end the meeting early.** "That meeting ended way too soon..." said no person, ever.

Bonus Hack: Worried your meetings are time-wasters? Link your calendar to your favorite AI tool (I've got instructions in your Surf Kit at THEJOBINSIDERS.COM/SURF) and then run it through this AI audit:

PROMPT

Analyze my calendar for the past two weeks and identify where I might be wasting time in meetings.

For each meeting, help me assess:

1. Could this have been an email, Slack message, or Loom video instead?

2. Are there people invited who don't need to be there?

3. Is the meeting longer than it needs to be?

4. If it's recurring, is it still serving a clear purpose?

5. Is there a clear agenda?

Then show me:

-Total hours I spent in meetings each week
-Estimated hours that could have been reclaimed with better meeting hygiene
-My top 3 specific recommendations for getting time back

Format your response as a prioritized action list, starting with the changes that would save the most time.

6. Thou Shalt Curate, Not Just Copy-and-Paste

Here's the scene that happens in every organization now:

> **Manager:** "Can you update me on the campaign performance?"
>
> **Non-conscientious teammate:** *Forwards 47-page analytics report.* "Here's all the data!"
>
> **Manager:** *Spends 2 hours digging through dashboards.* "What does this mean?"
>
> **Non-conscientious teammate:** "Umm…"

This is what I call the AI Data Dump - and it's killing careers everywhere.

Because here's what's happened: AI has made it easier than ever to generate content. Want a 100-slide presentation? ChatGPT can bang it out. Want every possible metric from your analytics? Click a button.

But the hard part - the valuable part - isn't generating information. **It's curating it into real insight.**

And so if you're just an AI Middleman - i.e., forwarding AI-generated slop without adding any real value - you're making yourself the perfect target for the next round of layoffs.

Here are three ways to avoid that trap:

1. **Don't dump data - provide insight.**

   > **Non-conscientious teammate:** "Here's our Q3 dashboard with 47 metrics"
   >
   > **Conscientious teammate:** "Out of all our Q3 metrics, one thing actually matters: our conversion rate dropped

15%. The root cause is mobile performance on iOS - which explains why Android conversions are actually up 8%. We need to decide whether to fix iOS or lean into Android."

See the difference?

The first approach adds no independent value from AI and leaves the recipient to do all the heavy lifting on their own.

The second approach does the curation work: identifies the *one* metric that matters, explains *why* it's happening, and tees-up a *real* action that can drive *real* results.

2. **Don't bring problems - bring solutions.**

Smart curation goes way beyond AI slop. Every time you surface an issue, your job is to also surface potential paths forward.

Non-conscientious teammate: "Our biggest client is unhappy with the latest release. What should we do?

Conscientious teammate: "Our biggest client is unhappy with the latest release - specifically the new UI. We can:

- (A) Revert to the old UI for just them (2 days work)
- (B) Fast-track the fixes they want into next sprint (1 week delay on other features)
- (C) Schedule a working session to customize the UI together (3 days + travel)

I recommend Option C because it builds the relationship and helps us learn what enterprise clients really need. Want me to set it up?"

Notice the pattern? **Problem + Options + Recommendation = Curation.**

Anyone can complain about a problem. But it takes a great teammate to figure out what to actually do about it!

3. **Don't write an epic - write a tweet.**

Mark Twain famously wrote: "I didn't have time to write a short letter, so I wrote a long one instead."

That was in 1871. And it's even more true today: It takes hard work and curation skill to write a concise message.

Consider these two approaches:

Non-conscientious teammate: "Hey! Hope you're having a great week. I wanted to reach out because I've been thinking about our Q4 strategy and had some thoughts I wanted to run by you. I know we talked about this briefly in last week's meeting, but I wasn't sure if we landed on a final decision. Anyway, I was reviewing the data from Q3 and noticed some interesting trends that might impact how we think about resource allocation for the next quarter. I think we should probably schedule some time to discuss this in more detail, but I wanted to get your initial thoughts first. Let me know when you have a chance to review the attached deck and we can set something up. Thanks!"

Conscientious teammate: "Can I please get your input on Q4 spending by Friday? Q3 data shows that the ROI on social media ads is starting to decrease, which suggests we should shift budget towards search engine marketing. Are you onboard with that strategy or should I schedule a 15-min call this week to decide?"

And just to make the stakes super clear, think about it this way: *Which teammate are you going to fight for the next time layoffs hit?*

The one who made you work just to figure out what they wanted? Or the one who respected your time enough to boil it down to the essentials:

- What's needed (your input)
- By when (Friday)
- Why it matters (Q3 data)
- What to do next (reply or quick chat)

So here's your rule, going forward: If you can't fit your messages into a tweet (280 characters), you haven't finished thinking.

Because even though every message doesn't need to be that short, if you can't potentially boil it down to that length, you don't understand it clearly enough to communicate it to anyone else.

Bonus Hack: Stop the AI Data Dump in its tracks with this prompt:

PROMPT

I'm about to send my boss this update:
[paste your draft]

Critique it ruthlessly:

1. Am I dumping data or providing insight?

2. Have I identified what actually matters vs. everything that's technically true?

3. Have I given them clear options and a recommendation?

4. Could I have made it more concise without giving up essential information?

5. Could they make a decision with JUST this update, or do they need to do more work?

7. Thou Shalt Take Shots on Goal, Not Just Talk About Them

Here's the uncomfortable truth: Most of us are spending way more time *preparing* to do work than actually *doing* work.

Strategy docs. Review sessions. Alignment meetings. Pre-reads for the pre-meeting before the actual meeting. We spend three weeks perfecting a plan, then two weeks getting everyone's input, then another week incorporating feedback - and by then, the market has already moved on.

It feels productive. Important. Strategic.

But it's actually just planning theater.

The solution? Only prioritize "shots on goal."

What's a shot on goal? Real work, out there in the real world, that has a real chance of moving the needle on your North Star. Not a doc about what you might do. Not a meeting to discuss what you could do. But **actual work that creates actual value for actual customers.**

Here's how to become the teammate who ships instead of just plans:

Distinguish between shots on goal and planning theater. Before you spend time on any activity, ask: "Is this a real shot on goal, or am I just planning?"

Shots on goal:

- Launching a beta feature to 100 users
- Building a prototype and getting customer feedback
- Making a sales call to a real prospect

Planning theater:

- Writing a 40-slide strategy deck
- Having a meeting to align on another meeting's agenda
- Asking for one more round of research before you dive in

The difference? Shots on goal create real value or real learning. Planning theater just creates more documents and meetings.

- **Apply the 70% rule.** Amazon has a famous principle: "Most decisions should probably be made with somewhere around 70% of the information you wish you had."[112] If you wait until you have 90% certainty, you're too late. The cost of delay outweighs the benefit of additional planning.

So when you're 70% confident in a direction, **take the shot.** Launch the experiment. Ship the feature. Make the decision. You can always adjust based on what you learn - and you'll learn infinitely more from doing than from planning.

- **Time-box your planning.** Never spend more time planning something than you're willing to spend doing it. If you're going to spend one week building something, spend one day planning it - not three weeks. If you're going to run a two-week experiment, spend two hours designing it - not two days.

  This forces you to focus on what actually matters. When you only have limited planning time, you can't perfectionist your way through every edge case. You have to identify the core questions and move forward.

- **Make action the default.** When you're in a meeting and someone says "We should think about doing X," immediately respond with: "What's the smallest version of X we could test this week?" Push for action, not more discussion.

  When you catch yourself saying "We need more data before we decide," ask: "What's the fastest way to get that data?" Often, the answer is to run a small test - not to schedule another research project.

---

112 Bezos, Jeff. "2016 Letter to Shareholders." *About Amazon*, April 16, 2017. https://www.aboutamazon.com/news/company-news/2016-letter-to-shareholders.

The goal isn't to be reckless. It's to recognize that one week of real-world testing teaches you more than one month of theoretical planning.

Bonus Hack: Want to make sure you're prioritizing shots on goal? Use this prompt:

🗣 PROMPT

```
Our North Star goal is: [your main objec-
tive]

Suggest 5 specific "shots on goals" (real
work that could get us closer to our North
Star) that will either lead directly to pow-
erful learning or, better yet, real results?
```

EXPERIMENTATION: TAKING OWNERSHIP INSTEAD OF JUST FOLLOWING ORDERS

Here's What I Did

Based on my earlier LinkedIn stories, you may have thought I was well on my way to the C-Suite there.

Not quite.

Let me tell you how my time at LinkedIn came to an abrupt end...

After two years of promotions and accolades, I was getting ready for our team's grand finale: The big launch of our flagship student products. To celebrate, Miranda asked me to create a video - just like the record-setting one we created at the start of my tenure. And so I figured: "No problem. I've done this before. I could do it in my sleep!"

But unlike the first time, where we hustled to find an amazing agency and push the boundaries of anything LinkedIn had ever done before, I decided that we could basically do this on autopilot: I hired a cheap agency in Kansas City. We made a decent video in a few weeks. It was fine, right?

And then I got invited to present it to the CEO.

Not just any CEO. Jeff Weiner - one of the most respected leaders in Silicon Valley, known for his exacting standards and ability to call out anyone's BS. Plus my boss, my boss's boss, and basically everyone who mattered at the company.

I walked into that conference room feeling confident. This was my moment to shine.

Thirty seconds into the video, Jeff stopped it.

"What is this?"

I froze.

"No really, what the f—k is this" he continued. "It's safe. It's forgettable. Why would any student care about this? How are you going to actually make this useful?"

The room went silent. All eyes turned to me.

"Ummm..." was my eloquent response.

Jeff proceeded to tear the video apart. Not mean-spirited, but surgical. Every assumption I'd made, every "best practice" I'd followed, every safe choice I'd made - he dismantled it all.

The meeting ended with no decision. No next steps. Just a room full of people who'd just watched me bomb the biggest presentation of my career.

That night, I was curled up in a fetal ball on our futon. My one-year-old daughter crawled over, puzzled by my catatonic state.

"Dada?"

"Ughhhhh..." was my best attempt at a reply.

The funk took weeks to lift. I'd wake up at 3 AM thinking: "Crap. It wasn't just a nightmare."

But once I got some distance from the pain, I had only one thought: **Never again.**

Never again would I play it safe. Never again would I just follow the formula. Never again would I settle for "perfectly adequate" when the situation demanded something extraordinary.

Because here's what I realized: Being agreeable and conscientious - that's necessary. But it's not sufficient.

You can be the nicest, most efficient teammate in the world. But if you're just maintaining the status quo, you're not actually creating value. You're just... existing.

The world doesn't need more people who can follow instructions. It needs people who can see what's not working and fix it - even when nobody told them to.

Fast Forward to 2025

I'm running The Job Insiders, and I need to hire a Virtual Assistant. Standard role - schedule meetings, manage email, basic administrative tasks.

I post the job. Get 200 applications.

And 197 of them look exactly the same.

Perfect grammar. Polished formatting. Impressive credentials. All clearly written by ChatGPT using the same prompts.

- *"I am writing to express my enthusiastic interest in the Virtual Assistant position..."*
- *"My extensive experience in administrative support, coupled with my passion for organizational excellence..."*
- *"I am confident that my skills align perfectly with your requirements..."*

They looked good on paper. But reading them, I had a sinking feeling of recognition.

These applicants were making the exact same mistake I'd made in that conference room with Jeff Weiner.

They were playing it safe. Following the formula. Creating something "perfectly adequate" that checked all the boxes but took zero risks.

They were optimizing to not get rejected - not to create something remarkable.

Then I got to application #198.

It was from Rose. And it was different.

Instead of generic corporate-speak, she wrote about **why** she wanted this specific role. She'd clearly researched The Job Insiders. She pointed out gaps in our content strategy and suggested specific improvements. She even questioned whether I was thinking too small about the role.

I brought her in for an interview, expecting a standard conversation about calendar management and email triage.

Instead, she challenged me: "Why aren't you getting your voice out there more? You've got this amazing expertise, but you're basically invisible online. If I'm going to help you, we need to think bigger than just scheduling."

I could hear Jeff's voice in my head: *"How are you actually going to make this better?"*

So I hired her on the spot.

What Rose did over the next year was the complete opposite of my safe, check-the-boxes approach that had failed so spectacularly:

1. **Where I had done just what my role required, Rose took ownership for the whole company.** She didn't just manage my calendar - she owned our entire outreach strategy, dramatically increasing calls with prospective clients. Not because it was in her job description, but because she saw what was needed.

2. **Where I had accepted that "good enough" was truly good enough, Rose questioned the status quo.** For instance, I assumed that launching a podcast was out of the question - after all, everyone knows that you need a whole team, a studio, and a big following. Or at least I assumed that until Rose built out a brand-new podcast for us from scratch!

3. **Where I waited to be told what to do, Rose just went out and got it done.** When I started writing this book, Rose didn't sit around waiting for detailed instructions. Instead, she put together a comprehensive digest of the latest AI research and provided detailed

feedback on each chapter - all while pushing me to think bigger about the book's potential impact.

The contrast between Rose and those 197 AI-generated applications - and between Rose and my younger self in that conference room - wasn't about credentials or experience.

It was about experimentation.

And because of that? I gave her actual ownership - a revenue share in the business. Because when someone acts like an owner, you make them one.

Here's What You Should Do

Experimentation isn't about being reckless or ignoring your manager's guidance. Instead, it's about doing exactly what your manager would do themselves - without having to be told first. Here are the three core commandments:

8. Thou Shalt Own the Biggest Challenges (Even When They're Not "Your Job")

Here's the career-limiting mindset that kills most people's potential:

- "That's not my job."
- "I'm just the [insert title here]."
- "Someone else owns that."

This mindset made sense in the Industrial Age, when jobs were clearly defined and managers told you exactly what to do.

But in the AI Age? It's a death sentence.

Because here's the honest truth: If your contribution is limited to doing *only* what you're told, AI can probably already do that exact thing better today.

So the question is no longer "Can you do your job description well?"

Instead, it's: "Can you see problems nobody *told* you to solve and fix them anyway?"

Here's what ownership actually looks like:

- **See beyond your title.** When Rose joined as a Virtual Assistant, she didn't limit herself to scheduling and email. She saw that our content strategy had gaps. She didn't wait to be promoted to "Content Strategist" before fixing them. She just... fixed them.

- **Treat company resources like your own.** In my very first job out of college, I was a lowly junior recruiter at Teach For America, making a whopping $26,000 a year in NYC! And yet, I remember discovering that we were paying AT&T $50,000 a year for phone service - as if it was 1967. So I asked a few of the new Voice-over-Internet phone companies for bids and it turned out that we could basically get the same service for next to nothing.

  While I was initially nervous to share what I discovered (after all, no young employee wants to have a senior leader screaming "Stay in your lane!"), I summoned up the courage to email the CFO. And you know what he said?

"Thanks for saving us $50K, Jeremy. I wish everyone here treated our money like it was *their own*."

- **Focus on what matters most.** Later in my career, I was hired as VP of Marketing at a hot edtech startup. The CEO, like most Silicon Valley CEOs, saw marketing as a way to look cool - like jazz hands for companies. And so he asked me to start by making a cool-looking video - just like that first one I made at LinkedIn!

There was only one problem: When I looked inside the company's CRM, there were no sales leads.

In other words, here we were contemplating a sexy sizzle reel... and the company was bleeding to death on the inside!

So promising the CEO that I'd "get to the video ASAP," I went off and built out a whole lead generation system instead. Not that I knew anything about these systems - but I knew enough to realize that, without them, that video was going to be played at our memorial service.

And so two months later, I presented our CEO our new $40 million sales pipeline - and no video. But suffice it to say, the idea of the video never came up again!

Bonus Hack: Want to find ownership opportunities hiding in plain sight? Use this prompt to discover where you can step up:

 **PROMPT**

Here's what I'm currently working on: [your projects and responsibilities]

Interview me to help identify ownership opportunities where I can go above and beyond, including:

1. What problems keep coming up that nobody seems to own?

2. What would make my boss's job significantly easier?

3. What's broken/inefficient that people have just accepted as "how things are"?

4. What could I start doing now that would create disproportionate value?

5. Where am I uniquely positioned to make an impact that others can't?

For each opportunity, suggest:

- The smallest first step I could take this week
- What success would look like
- How to communicate my initiative without seeming presumptuous

9. Thou Shalt Interrogate Sacred Cows

Every organization has sacred cows - the things "we've always done this way" that everyone's afraid to question:

- "We always use this vendor."
- "We always have this meeting."
- "We always follow this process."
- "We always require three rounds of approval before launch."

Here's what sacred cows really are: **Legacy decisions that made sense once but nobody's bothered to revisit.**

And in the AI age, where change happens faster than ever, sacred cows become expensive liabilities.

The teammates who thrive? They're the ones willing to ask the uncomfortable questions:

- "Why do we do it this way?"
- "What problem was this solving originally?"
- "Is that problem still relevant?"
- "What would happen if we stopped?"

Here's how to interrogate sacred cows without getting trampled:

- **Start with genuine curiosity, not criticism.** There's a massive difference between:

   ✘ "This weekly status email is a waste of time."

   ✔ "Help me understand - what problem does the weekly status email solve? Is there a more efficient way to achieve that outcome?"

   The first one makes people defensive. The second one invites collaboration.

- **Look for "because we've always done it that way."** That phrase is a giant red flag. It means nobody remembers why the decision was made, but everyone's too scared to change it.

  Research from Stanford and UC-Berkeley shows that organizations often continue practices long after their original justification has disappeared - a phenomenon they call "organizational inertia."[113]

  When you hear "because we've always done it that way," you've found a sacred cow. Time to start asking questions.

- **Run small experiments, not revolutions.** You don't need to kill the sacred cow immediately. Just test whether it's actually necessary.

  For example, at Khan Academy, we had a sacred cow called the Channel Review Meeting. Every single month, each of the six channel marketers had to spend five hours gathering all of their data in advance of the meeting - even though the data never changed much. And then six more people, all the way up to the VP of Marketing, had to sit there and listen in silence for another hour. Nobody remembered why it started, but everyone showed up.

  I didn't cancel it immediately. Instead, I said: "Let's try skipping it for a month. If anything breaks, we'll bring it back."

---

113 Hannan, Michael T., and John Freeman. 1984. "Structural Inertia and Organizational Change." *American Sociological Review* 49 (2): 149–164. https://www.jstor.org/stable/2095567.

Nothing broke. We killed the sacred cow and got back dozens of hours of everyone's time each month.

Bonus Hack: Want to identify sacred cows in your organization? Use this prompt (which, similar to the meeting prompt, is enhanced by giving AI access to your routines):

 PROMPT

Look through my emails, calendar, and files to help me identify potential sacred cows by:

1. Flagging anything that's been happening for 6+ months without change

2. Identifying activities that don't seem to have a clear value

3. Suggesting low-risk experiments to test whether each activity is actually necessary

4. Proposing alternative approaches that might achieve the same outcome more efficiently

10. Thou Shalt Do It Now, Not When You're Told (Which Is Too Late)

Here's the hardest truth about being a great teammate in the AI age:

By the time someone tells you to do something, you should have already done it.

Wait, isn't that impossible?

No. It's called **being proactive.**

And it's one of the most valuable habits you can develop - because it's the one thing AI fundamentally cannot do.

AI is brilliant at following instructions. It's great at delivering results as soon as you ask. But when was the last time it anticipated your needs? Or went out and got something done for you?

Exactly.

Being proactive is your existential edge.

Here's what it actually looks like:

- **Notice patterns before they become problems.** Rose didn't wait for me to say "Our sales funnel is running a little low." She noticed the pattern, diagnosed the issue, and had solutions ready before I even knew there was a problem.

  Research from organizational psychology shows that proactive employees - those who identify and solve problems before being asked - are rated as significantly higher performers and are more likely to be promoted.[114]

- **Create clarity from ambiguity.** Most people hate ambiguous situations. "I don't know what to do, so I'll wait for clearer instructions."

---

114 Seibert, Scott E., Maria L. Kraimer, and Robert C. Liden. 2001. "A Social Capital Theory of Career Success." *Academy of Management Journal* 44 (2): 219–237. https://journals.aom.org/doi/10.5465/3069452.

Great teammates embrace ambiguity. They see it as permission to figure out the right answer instead of waiting to be told.

When I told Rose "We should probably do a podcast... you know, at some point... eventually," that was pretty darn ambiguous. And so she could have easily responded with: "Great! Let me know when *you* want to start."

Instead, she researched podcast formats, identified potential guests, outlined topics, and came back with: "Here's a complete plan for our first season. If you approve, I can have episode one ready to record in two weeks."

- **Do what needs to be done, not just what's in your job description.** When I was 18, working the register at Walgreens on a quiet Tuesday afternoon, an elderly woman shuffled up with a single pint of ice cream. Her hands were shaking as she counted out exact change. The line was empty - I had nothing else to do. And I noticed she was struggling to carry both her cane and the ice cream.

So I offered to help her to her car. "Oh no, sweetheart, you don't have to do that," she protested. But it was 95 degrees outside and that ice cream was already starting to melt. So I walked her out, loaded it into her trunk, and came back inside.

Where my assistant manager was waiting. Arms crossed. Face red. "What the hell do you think you're doing? That's not your job. Your job is to stay at the register."

But here's what he didn't understand: **The job isn't the job description. The job is doing what needs to be done.**

And even though I've fallen into that job description trap at times - as with the video incident - most of my success has been from seeing the bigger picture. From coming back to that North Star of doing what's right and what needs to be done. And then getting it frickin' done - no questions asked.

Bonus Hack: Want to build your proactive chops? Try this prompt:

 **PROMPT**

You are my Proactivity Coach.

Based on my role and responsibilities - [insert here] - help me spot opportunities to act before I'm asked:

1. Ask me clarifying questions about my team, goals, and recurring problems.

2. Identify patterns that might become future issues or missed opportunities.

3. Turn vague ideas or ambiguous requests into concrete proposals.

> 4. Suggest 5-10 proactive actions beyond my job description that would create clear value, ordered by impact.

READY FOR WHAT'S NEXT?

You now have the playbook for becoming an indispensable teammate: Be agreeable, be conscientious, be willing to experiment.

Master these ten commandments, and you'll always have opportunities.

But what if traditional employment isn't the only path forward?

What if there was a way to build a career that's even more resilient to AI disruption - one where you're not dependent on any single employer or job market?

That's exactly what we'll explore in the next chapter.

9

HOW TO BUILD YOUR NEXT JOB

t's 2012, and I'm sitting in my new apartment in Mountain View, California, staring at my laptop.

I'd finally made it. After seven years of failed applications and rejections, I'd landed my dream job at LinkedIn. Good salary. Amazing perks. The kind of role that made my parents proudly tell their friends about their son in Silicon Valley.

But I couldn't shake this nagging feeling in my gut.

What if LinkedIn decides they don't need me anymore? What if the company gets acquired and my role gets eliminated? What if I want to do something different but I'm locked into this one career path?

I'd spent seven years trying to get *just one* tech company to give me a chance. And now that I finally had what I wanted, I realized something terrifying:

All my eggs were now in that *one* basket. Which meant my entire career depended on someone else's decision to keep employing me.

So I made a decision that seemed crazy at the time: I was going to build **my own thing** on the side.

Not quit my job, mind you (after all, I'd fought too hard just to get there!). But slowly, methodically, deliberately I was going to build something that could give me options.

I started with the simplest possible first step: A self-published book about cover letters. Don't feel like you need to start with a fancy, VC-backed startup. My very first entrepreneurial venture was a short e-book written on my phone while flying cross-country!

Why?

Because I'd just spent seven years writing hundreds of them - so it was something I had become an expert at (i.e., it wouldn't require years of additional research). Plus, by building on top of Amazon's existing Kindle platform, I wouldn't have to build up a massive audience on my own.

So how'd it go?

The first year, I made $7.35. **Total.**

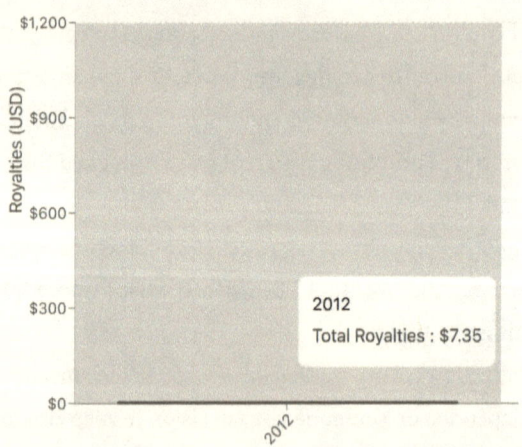

Ouch.

My friends thought I was wasting my time. "You work at LinkedIn - just focus on your career there," they said.

But I kept going. I spent mornings before work reaching out to journalists writing about careers. Evenings after work responding to reader questions. Weekends refining the book based on feedback.

The second year? About $1,000.

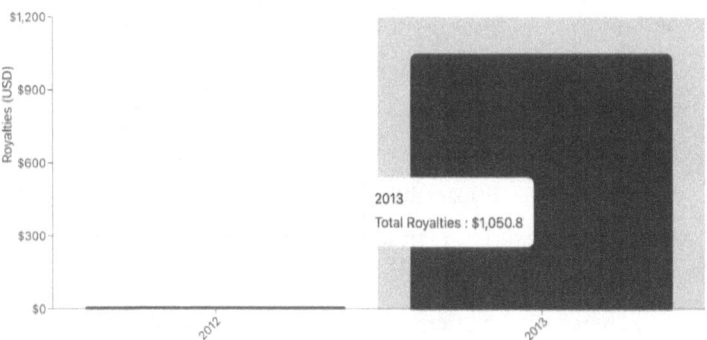

A little better than "ouch" - but still making about $2.50/hour.

Still basically nothing. But it was *something*. Proof that I could create value outside of LinkedIn's walls.

So I expanded. I built an online course, teaching people how to land jobs in Silicon Valley. Same principle: Package up what I'd learned the hard way and help others skip the seven years of rejection I'd endured.

Year three? $16,230.

Not enough to quit. Not even close. But enough to prove I was onto something.

By year seven, I was making $50,000/year on the side. Still working at tech companies full-time, but now with a safety net. Real money. Real proof that I could create value independently.

Then COVID hit. And everything changed.

I started teaching virtual LinkedIn workshops to MBAs and other students who were stuck at home. And then, when ChatGPT came out, I added AI training for hundreds of universities around the world.

Suddenly I wasn't just making a few thousands on the side. I was making meaningful income. The kind of income that made quitting my full-time job not just possible, but obvious.

In 2024 - twelve years after earning $7.35 for a year's worth of effort - I finally did it. I left my corporate job and went all-in on my business.

But here's what matters most: I didn't *have* to wait twelve years. I *chose* to.

Because once I had that side income flowing, I wasn't trapped anymore. I could stay at my day job because I *wanted* to, not because I *had* to. And when the time was right - when the portfolio income was strong enough and I was genuinely ready - I made the transition on my terms.

That's the power of a portfolio career. Not just multiple income streams, but multiple forms of freedom that make you antifragile - not just resilient to disruption, but actually stronger when it hits.

And here's the timing that matters for you: If I could build this starting in 2012 with just determination and a self-published book, it's exponentially easier today with AI as your co-founder.

You don't need to wait twelve years like I did. In fact, you can get started today - in the time it takes to finish this chapter.

THE DEATH OF THE SINGLE-TRACK CAREER
(And Why That's Actually Good News)

Here's the career advice I got, growing up in blue-collar Buffalo, NY: Get a good job. Work hard. Climb the ladder. Retire with a pension.

It turns out that world is now dead.

And AI just delivered the final blow.

Here's why: The old career model assumed that landing one good job meant stability for years - maybe decades. You'd build expertise in one domain, climb the ranks, and your specialized knowledge would protect you.

But in the AI age, that specialized knowledge is becoming commoditized faster than ever. According to the World Economic Forum, the half-life of a learned skill has dropped from 30 years in 1984 to just four years today.[115]

Think about what that means: If you spend four years getting a degree in a specific field, half of what you learned is already outdated by the time you graduate.

The single-track career isn't just risky. It's a ticking time bomb.

But here's the good news: The same AI that's disrupting traditional employment is also making it easier than ever to build alternative career paths.

Consider what AI has democratized:

---

115 Emeritus. "The Half-life of Skills." *Emeritus Blog*. Accessed December 2, 2025. https://emeritus.org/blog/the-half-life-of-skills/.

- **Software development:** You used to need to hire a $150K engineer to build an app. Now you can use tools like Cursor or Lovable to build whole applications with plain English.
- **Marketing:** You used to need an agency charging $10K/month. Now you can use AI to write copy, design graphics, analyze campaigns, and optimize ads.
- **Content creation:** You used to need a production team. Now you can use AI to research, draft, edit, and even create audio/video content.
- **Business operations:** You used to need multiple employees. Now AI can handle customer service, bookkeeping, scheduling, and project management.

The barriers to starting something on your own have never been lower. Which means the traditional calculation - "I need to find a stable job because starting my own thing is too risky" - has completely flipped.

Now the calculation is: "Depending entirely on one employer might be the biggest risk of all."

THE PORTFOLIO CAREER ADVANTAGE

But let's be clear about what we're talking about here. A portfolio career isn't about "hustling" or working 80-hour weeks or becoming some kind of solopreneur superhero.

It's about strategic diversification.

Think of it like investing. You wouldn't put 100% of your savings in a single stock - that would be reckless. So why put 100% of your income-generating capacity in a single employer?

A portfolio career means building multiple streams of value creation that:

1. Leverage your core strengths (from Chapter 3)

You're not starting from scratch or chasing random opportunities. You're building on the ikigai foundation you already identified.

2. Combine human + AI skills (from Chapters 4-5)

You're not competing with AI or getting replaced by it. You're using it to amplify what you do best while maintaining the human judgment that creates real value.

3. Compound over time (from Chapter 6)

Each project builds your skills, reputation, and network. The second thing you build is easier than the first. The third is easier than the second.

And here's the beautiful part: You already have a head start.

Remember that micro-entrepreneurial project you started building in Chapter 4? The one where you interviewed users, created compelling content, and led people to take action?

That wasn't just a learning exercise.

That was the seed of your portfolio career.

THE SPF FRAMEWORK: FROM SIDE PROJECT TO REAL INCOME

To start growing that seed into something more sustainable, I'm going to teach you my SPF Framework - a systematic way to turn your existing project into real income, starting today.

Because just like surfers need sun protection to stay out on the water longer, you need the right SPF to layer on top of your existing SURF foundation!

The SPF Framework has three components:

S **Skills:** What valuable skills can you sell?

P **Product:** How should you package them?

F **Foundation:** What tools make it easiest to start?

Let's break down each component - and for each one, I'll show you exactly what I did, then give you the playbook to do the same.

SKILLS: WHAT CAN YOU SELL?

Here's What I Did

When I started thinking about building something on the side, I asked myself a simple question: *What do I know how to do that other people struggle with?*

The answer was obvious - painfully obvious, given the seven years I'd spent figuring it out.

Getting a job was my superpower.

Not in some abstract "I'm good at careers" way. I mean the specific, tactical, in-the-trenches work of:

- Writing cover letters that actually got responses
- Optimizing resumes to get past Applicant Tracking Systems
- Networking my way into opportunities that weren't posted online
- Interviewing in a way that made Hiring Managers say yes

I'd failed at all of this for years before I finally cracked the code. And that painful learning curve? That was my unfair advantage. I could help others skip the mistakes I'd made.

Here's What You Should Do

Go back to the ikigai map you created in Chapter 3. You identified your core strengths - the things you're better at than most people, that energize you, and that the world actually needs.

Now ask yourself: *Which of those strengths would someone actually pay me to help them with?*

Use this prompt to identify your monetizable strengths:

PROMPT

Based on my core strengths and energizers, what are 5 specific ways I could sell my expertise to people who need it?

My top strengths: [from your ikigai map]

What energizes me: [from your ikigai map]

For each pathway, suggest:

- What specific problem it solves?
- Who would pay for this?
- Why they'd pay for it instead of figuring it out themselves?

AI OUTPUT

Based on the strengths revealed in your LinkedIn recommendations — expertise, empathy, mentorship, energy, and communication — here are **five high-leverage ways to sell your expertise**, framed around who pays, what pain it solves, and why they buy rather than DIY.

1. Career Branding Accelerator for Professionals

Problem Solved:
Mid-career professionals struggle to differentiate themselves on LinkedIn and in interviews; they need a clear, confident narrative that aligns with their goals.

Who Pays:
Mid- to senior-level professionals seeking job transitions, promotions, or visibility in new industries (especially tech, consulting, or academia).

Why They Pay:
You blend insider knowledge of LinkedIn algorithms and recruiting psychology with storytelling expertise — something most people can't replicate through generic online tips. Clients pay for personalized, evidence-based branding that yields faster callbacks and recruiter outreach.

The first step is the hardest one. Don't get pegged to perfection - instead, just get going!

Here's what this might look like for our three example projects:

Sustainability-Focused Data Analyst
- *Skill:* Translating complex climate data into actionable steps
- *Who pays:* Community organizations, nonprofits, local governments
- *Why they pay:* They have access to data but no one who can make it meaningful for non-experts

EdTech Marketer

- *Skill:* Identifying which classroom technologies actually work vs. which are hype
- *Who pays:* School technology coordinators, district IT leaders
- *Why they pay:* They're drowning in options and need expert curation

Engineering Leader

- *Skill:* Helping technical managers lead teams without losing their engineering credibility
- *Who pays:* New engineering managers, tech leads
- *Why they pay:* Most leadership advice doesn't account for the unique challenges of managing technical teams

As with all great businesses from Apple to Zappos, you don't want to start with a generic product for generic customers. Instead, you're starting with a clear focus: Selling *specific* expertise that solves *specific* problems for *specific* people.

PRODUCT: HOW SHOULD YOU PACKAGE IT?

Here's What I Did

Once I knew my monetizable superpower was helping people land jobs, I had to figure out how to package that expertise. After all, people don't just buy raw skills - they want a defined product or service with a bow on top!

And so I realized there were four existing package models for career support:

1. Books
2. Courses
3. Trainings
4. Coaching

I started with the simplest one: a $2.99 Kindle book. No complicated videography set-ups. No hunting for clients online. Just packaging what I knew into a format that was dead simple to deliver.

Then, as my audience grew, so did I. Books led to courses. Courses led to training programs for universities. Training programs led to coaching for executives who wanted personalized attention.

Each format was tailored to my evolving audience - and for me as an evolving entrepreneur. I only added complexity to my offering mix when my customers demanded it - and I was ready to handle it.

Here's What You Should Do

There are really only four main ways to package your expertise:

1. Services (You do the work for them)
- *Examples:* Consulting, freelancing, done-for-you services
- *Pros:* Highest prices, immediate feedback from clients
- *Cons:* Hardest to scale, most time-intensive

2. Coaching (You guide them to do the work)

- *Examples:* 1-on-1 coaching, group coaching, workshops
- *Pros:* High prices, direct impact, flexible delivery
- *Cons:* Still trading time for money, requires strong facilitation skills

3. Content (You teach them to do the work)

- *Examples:* Books, online courses, newsletters
- *Pros:* Scalable, can reach many people, recurring revenue potential
- *Cons:* Requires upfront creation time, harder to differentiate

4. Products (You create a tool they use)

- *Examples:* Templates, workbooks, software
- *Pros:* Highly scalable, can be sold globally
- *Cons:* Usually lower prices, more technical skills required

Use this prompt to choose your packaging:

 PROMPT

> Based on the following ways to merchandise my skills, which product format makes the most sense for me to start with?
>
> Make your recommendation (including a suggested price) based on the following considerations:

- What can I launch in the next 30 days?
- What requires the least upfront investment?
- What lets me learn from customers fastest?

[Insert options from the first step]

 **AI OUTPUT**

Recommended Starting Format

🎓 Live Virtual Workshop: "AI-Powered LinkedIn Branding for Career Growth"

Suggested Price:

- **$49–$99 per attendee** (individual ticket)

or

- **$500–$1,000 per private group session** (for universities or small teams)

Why This Format Makes the Most Sense

1. Fast to Launch (Under 30 Days)
You can host this via Zoom or Google Meet with no web development, marketing automation, or content recording required.

People buy products, not expertise. So put your skills in a form that people can actually buy!

Here's what I recommend for each of our example projects:

Sustainability-Focused Data Analyst
- *Start with:* 60-minute data training workshop for local environmental nonprofits ($200/workshop)
- *Why:* Organizations already have budgets for workshops, you can deliver it immediately, and you get instant feedback

EdTech Marketer
- *Start with:* 30-minute tech audit calls ($50/call)
- *Why:* School IT leaders are used to paying for professional development, the commitment is small, and you can do multiple sessions in a week

Engineering Leader
- *Start with:* Paid newsletter ($10/month)
- *Why:* Your audience is already on Substack, you're already creating content, and you can start monetizing immediately

Notice the pattern? Start with whatever is:

- **Fastest to launch** (days, not months)
- **Easiest to deliver** (uses skills you already have)
- **Lowest risk for buyers** (small commitment, clear value)

You can always expand to other formats later. In fact, that's exactly what you should do - which we'll cover in the expansion section below.

FOUNDATION: WHAT TOOLS MAKE IT EASY?

Here's What I Did

For each of my four product formats, I chose a single tech tool that made it ridiculously easy to get started:

- **Books → Kindle Direct Publishing** – I literally just uploaded a Word document. No design skills needed. No upfront costs. Amazon handled everything.
- **Courses → Thinkific** – Set it up in an afternoon. Free to start. They handle payments, course delivery, everything.
- **Trainings → Zoom** – Universities and companies already use it. No friction. I just showed up and taught.
- **Coaching → Calendly** – People book themselves on my calendar, they pay to confirm the appointment, done.

That's it. Four tools. Each one took less than two hours to set up. And note what's not required:

- A fancy website
- Months developing a brand
- Hiring an expensive developer or designer

Instead, I picked the simplest tool for each format and started selling.

Here's What You Should Do

Here's my opinionated guide to the best starting tools for each format:

For Services:

- **Upwork**: Clients are already looking for your skills (it's the world's largest freelancing site) + built-in payment processing
- **Fiverr**: A smaller site but easier to get started since people just buy your skills directly vs. a whole bidding process

For Coaching:

- **Calendly**: Easiest tool to get started with - can even accept payments directly
- **Acuity:** Provides more advanced features like recurring appointments and group classes

For Content:

Books

- **Amazon Kindle Direct Publishing**: Dead simple for both e-books and print + access to the world's largest online marketplace
- **Draft2Digital**: If you want to escape the Amazon ecosystem, this distribution aggregator gets your book into Apple Books, Kobo, Barnes & Noble, and library systems

Courses

- **Udemy**: If you don't have an audience, this is a great place to start since it's the biggest marketplace for online courses
- **Thinkific**: If you already have access to potential customers and want to keep all of the proceeds from your sales, this gives you everything you need - from course creation to marketing tools - in one place

Newsletters

- **Medium**: If you're willing to sacrifice control for access to new readers, this gives you immediate exposure at the cost of not owning the relationship with your subscribers
- **Substack**: If you already have a small tribe to start with, this lets you have a more direct relationship and maximize your subscription revenue

For Products:

- **Gumroad**: The easiest way to start selling templates, workbooks, and any kind of digital tool
- **Etsy**: Even though it's best-known known for crafts, it's also a massive marketplace for digital downloads - from planner pages and digital journals to branding kits and resume templates

Use this prompt to pick your foundation:

PROMPT

Based on my chosen product, what's the absolute simplest tech stack I need to launch in the next 7 days?

Suggest:

- The best platform(s) that cover set-up, customer discovery, and checkout (with preference for all-in-one solutions)

- Exact steps to get set up

- What I can skip for now

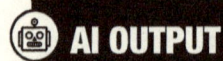

AI OUTPUT

☑ **Why Thinkific Is a Smart "All-in-One" Platform for You**

- Thinkific lets you build, price, deliver, and manage courses/workshops under one roof.

- The interface is beginner-friendly: drag-and-drop course builder, easy upload for video/PDF/slide content, and built-in sales/checkout flow.

- It supports digital products, memberships, and communities — giving

> you flexibility in how you expand later.
>
> • Because it handles your "course site + checkout + student access + hosting", you avoid needing a separate website or complex e-commerce stack.
>
> For your first offer, Thinkific hits the sweet spot between simplicity, professionalism, and scalability.

What's the fastest way to speed through the Entrepreneurship Tech Trap? Let AI do the research for you - and then just go!

Here's a complete Foundation for each example project:

Data Analyst's Sustainability Workshop

- **Calendly:** Schedule workshops + collect money
- **Google Docs:** Presentation + handouts
- **Setup time:** 5 hours (draft presentation + set-up Calendly)
- **Cost:** $10/month

EdTech Marketer's Tech Audit Calls

- **Calendly:** Schedule calls + collect money
- **Zoom:** Video conference
- **Setup time:** 2 hours (set-up Calendly and integrate with Zoom)
- **Cost:** $23/month

Engineering Leadership Newsletter

- **Substack:** Distribute content + handle subscriptions
- **Gemini:** Research + image generation
- **Setup time:** 10 hours (set-up Substack and create the first few posts)
- **Cost:** $20/month + 10% of subscription revenue

The key principle: **Use as few tools as possible.** Every additional tool is another thing to learn, maintain, and debug.

I see too many people spend months building the "perfect" tech stack and never launching. Don't be that person.

Pick one platform. Set it up today. Launch this week.

"BUT WHAT ABOUT…" (AKA COMMON FEARS)

Before we move on to your launch plan, let's address the fears I hear most often:

"But I don't have time for a side project."

You're not training for a marathon here. The SPF Framework requires maybe five hours per week to get started. That's one Netflix episode per night.

The question isn't whether you have time. It's whether you're willing to trade passive consumption for active creation.

"But what if I fail?"

Define failure. If you build something, learn skills, make some money, and meet interesting people - is that failure?

The only way you actually fail is by not trying - and staying 100% dependent on someone else's decision to employ you.

"But my idea isn't special enough."

My first idea was a frickin' cover letter book! There were literally 40,000+ existing products in this space on Amazon:

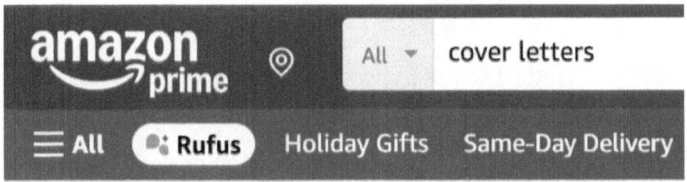

1-48 of over 40,000 results for "cover letters"

Competition isn't a sign you can't win - it's a sign that you can!

And yet, the sheer number of existing products was proof that this was a real problem worth tackling - especially if I could provide a real solution to the people who needed it.

Remember: Your idea doesn't have to be revolutionary. *It has to be helpful.*

"But I'm not an entrepreneur type."

Neither was I. I was a kindergarten teacher who liked structure and stability.

The portfolio career isn't about becoming Steve Jobs. It's about taking the skills you already have and packaging them in a way that creates value.

You've already proven you can do this in Chapters 4-5. This is just the next evolution.

"But what about [insert specific objection]?"

Here's the truth: There will always be a reason to wait. To not start. To play it safe.

But playing it safe - betting everything on one employer in an AI-disrupted world - is actually the riskiest move of all.

YOUR 7-DAY LAUNCH PLAN

Alright, enough planning. You've got your Skills, Product, and Foundation figured out.

Now it's time to actually launch something.

Here's your exact 7-day plan:

Day 1: Set Up Your Foundation

Start by getting your tech set-up. And don't worry about putting down a little money for a subscription to Calendly or Zoom. Just like signing-up for a gym membership creates a certain amount of healthy guilt, getting some skin in the game early can compel you to take the plunge when you're thinking about turning back!

And most importantly, don't fall into the trap of Wantrepreneurship - in other words, procrastinating on the stuff that really *matters* by focusing on all the things that really *don't*. For instance, one of the reasons it took me so long to reach escape velocity with my side hustle is that I kept getting side-tracked by all the trappings of entrepreneurship:

- "Here's my shiny, new website" (10 visitors/month)
- "Here are my sexy, laser-cut business cards" (handed out five times)
- "Here are all the clever domain names I bought!" (used zero times)

So avoid that trap and keep your eyes on the prize: Just the bare minimum tech you need for liftoff.

Days 2-4: Create Your MVP

Not your "Most Valuable Player" - your Minimum Viable Product. In other words, take all the skills you've already developed in the preceding chapters and bang out just enough to have something to offer:

- **For services:** Create your first Upwork or Fiverr listing - outlining the problem you're tackling, how you can solve it, and why clients should believe in you
- **For coaching:** Create a Calendly scheduling calendar that describes what a coaching session entails, what clients need to share ahead of time, and what they can expect afterwards
- **For content:** Create an outline of the overall product and then write the first chapter, lesson, or newsletter
- **For products:** Create your first draft of the product and upload it to Gumroad or Etsy

When I first started selling online courses, I spent nearly a year building a course that was absolutely amazing... except for the fact that no one actually wanted it! So avoid spending months creating the "perfect" product that no one wants - and, instead, start with just the essential content required to test out your idea.

Day 5: Announce to Your Tribe

Remember everyone who engaged with your project back in Chapters 4-6? Send them this:

Subject: [your offer name] - Now Available

Hi [name],

Remember when you [specific engagement with your past project]?

Based on that feedback, I've created [your offer] to help [specific outcome].

For just the first 10 customers, I'm offering it for [price] and including [specific deliverable].

Interested? Just reply "YES" and I'll send details.

Thanks for inspiring me!

[your name]

Note that this is NOT the time to focus on profit maximization. Your ideal price should be above $0 (because you want your customers to have skin in the game) but well below the regular market price (because you want to maximize the number of people who opt-in and, hence, your learning).

Days 6-7: Deliver and Get Feedback

Deliver your MVP to your first customers - be it the first step of the service, the first coaching session, the first chapter/lesson/newsletter, or the first draft of your product.

But before you go back to complete the rest of the steps, sessions, or content, be sure to take a temperature check on the following:

- What was most valuable?
- What confused you?
- What would make this worth 2X the price?

That way, when you sit down to extend your offering, you're not flying blind. Because you now have visibility into exactly what your market needs - which means the next step, session, or chapter can be way more effective.

That's how you go from $7 to $7,000 in months - not years!

GROWING OVER TIME: HORIZONTAL AND VERTICAL EXPANSION

Once you've launched and started to learn from your audience, you have two clear paths to grow:

Horizontal Expansion: New Audiences

This is what I did when I went from selling my career courses to individual job seekers to licensing them to universities.

Because by collecting candid feedback from my original audience, I learned two things:

1. There was a real **need** for effective career advice
2. But, ironically, job-seekers make for challenging customers since they often lacked both the **ability to pay** and **recurring demand** (i.e., once you get a job, ideally you won't be looking again for a long, long time!)

Whereas I discovered that universities had both:

1. The **need** - since career outcomes are the #1 reason students cite for attending college[116]
2. But also the **ability to pay** and the **recurring demand** (since each new year brings in a whole new cohort)

So I made the switch. But notice that I didn't change the foundational Skill or even the Product - just the audience.

Here's a prompt you can use to identify your own horizontal opportunities that tap into that trifecta of audience characteristics:

 **PROMPT**

> I currently sell [your offer] to [your audience].
>
> What are 5 other audiences who need the same product, have the ability to pay, and have recurring demand?

---

116 Auter, Zac. "Half of College Students Say Their Major Leads to a Good Job." *Gallup News Service*, January 16, 2018. https://news.gallup.com/poll/225446/half-college-students-say-major-leads-good-job.aspx.

For each audience, suggest:

- Who they are, specifically?
- Why they'd need my product?
- Whether and how I'd need to repackage my offer?
- What price point makes sense?

 AI OUTPUT

1. Corporate Outplacement Programs

Who they are
Companies that lay off employees and pay for external support (career coaching, job-search training) to help them land new roles.

Why they need your product
Outplacement services are expensive; many firms want lower-cost, scalable alternatives that still deliver strong results. Your course is plug-and-play and helps protect employer brand during layoffs.

Do you need to repackage?
Yes – bundle as an **Enterprise Outplacement Package**, with:

- Seats for laid-off employees
- Progress dashboards
- Optional live Q&A sessions

Price point

- **$300-$1,000 per employee**, depending on volume and support. Outplacement budgets are usually strong, and HR tends to renew contracts annually.

Your first audience is just that - your first, but very likely not your last. Chances are if you can generate real value for one group, you can do it for another!

Example: Data Analyst's Sustainability Workshop

- *Current:* $200 workshops for local nonprofits
- *Horizontal options:*
  - Corporate sustainability teams ($2,000 training day)
  - University environmental programs ($5,000 semester partnership)
  - Local government planning departments ($3,000 consultation package)

Notice: Same core skill (making climate data actionable). Different audiences. 5-25X higher prices.

Vertical Expansion:
Same Audience, Higher Value

Once I had switched to serving universities, I realized I was barely scratching the surface of their need.

While my amazing career center partners were happy to share my online courses with their students, what they really needed were *live* workshops. Especially after COVID shutdowns led to complaints that students were paying six-figures to essentially watch videos online, delivering live and engaging sessions became paramount.

Once I finally awoke to this need, I realized that I could better serve my partners with a full menu of offerings - everything from course licenses for less than $1K to in-person presentations and keynotes for 10X that amount:

Online Courses
$999

Live Webinar
$1,999

Courses + Webinar
~~$3K~~ $2,499

In-Person Speaking
$9,999

Menus aren't just for restaurants!

To figure out that menu for your audience, start with the key principle: Once someone trusts you enough to buy your basic offer, some percentage will want to go deeper.

So your menu might look like:

Entry point (Low price, low touch) → **Core offer** (Medium price, medium touch) → **Premium offer** (High price, high touch)

Here's a prompt to get started:

PROMPT

I currently sell [your offer] at [price] to [audience].

Design a 3-tier value ladder around the underlying goal of the offering - but feel free to update the offering to match each tier:

- Entry tier: Lower price and lower touch
- Core tier: Mid-price and mid-touch
- Premium tier: Higher price and higher touch

For each tier, specify exactly what's included and why someone would choose it.

AI OUTPUT

Tier 1 – Entry: "Career Foundations Toolkit"

Price Range: ~$199–$399 per site license (low price, low touch)

What's Included

- **Self-paced online career modules** (e.g., résumé basics, interviewing fundamentals, LinkedIn essentials).

- **Downloadable student templates** (résumé templates, cover letters, networking scripts).

- **Monthly pre-recorded workshop** on a rotating "Career Skills Topic of the Month."

- **Basic admin dashboard** for the career center (student usage reporting, basic analytics).

- **Email support only** (48-72 hour response).

Why Career Centers Choose This Tier

- They need a **budget-friendly, scalable curriculum** to supplement staff.

- Ideal for centers with **limited staff bandwidth** or those wanting to **test your content** before committing to a deeper partnership.

- Works well for centers seeking **on-demand resources** to give students "just-in-time" support during peak seasons.

Having a hard time seeing the possibilities? AI can often give you a broader sense of what's possible than just our intuitions alone.

Example: EdTech Marketer's Tech Audit

- *Entry tier:* Free 5-minute tech stack auto-recommender ($0, leads to paid offers)
- *Core tier:* 30-minute audit call ($50, current offer)
- *Premium tier:* 90-day implementation package ($500, includes audit + 3 monthly check-ins + email support)

The magic happens when you combine both:

1. Start with one audience and one product
2. Add vertical tiers (entry, core, premium)
3. Then replicate horizontally to new audiences
4. Then add vertical tiers for those audiences too

That's how $50/month becomes $500/month becomes $5,000/month - not through working harder, but through expanding strategically.

WHAT BUILDING YOUR OWN JOB REALLY MEANS

Here's what I want you to understand about portfolio careers:

This isn't about becoming an entrepreneur or quitting your job or building a million-dollar business.

It's about developing one of the most important skills in the AI age: **The ability to create value** *independently*.

When you can do that - when you've proven to yourself that you can package your expertise, find customers, deliver results, and get paid - you become fundamentally *unbreakable*.

Not because you have one stable job. But because you've developed the meta-skill that lets you create jobs for yourself, again and again, no matter what the market does.

Some people will use this to eventually go full-time. Others will keep it as meaningful side income forever. Others will use it as a safety net while they climb the traditional career ladder.

All of those are wins.

Because the real value isn't the money you make or the customers you serve.

It's the confidence you gain from knowing: *"I can create value. I can make money. I don't need anyone's permission to do work that matters."*

BUT THERE'S ONE SKILL THAT MATTERS EVEN MORE

Here's what I've learned from 15+ years watching people succeed (and fail) in tech:

The people who truly thrive - the ones who not only survive disruption but actually get stronger because of it - have one thing in common.

It's not technical skills. It's not even being a great teammate.

It's something deeper. Something that makes all the other skills possible.

It's the unshakeable belief that they control their own destiny.

They don't wait for permission. They don't blame circumstances. They don't let setbacks define them.

When AI disrupts their industry, they adapt. When a job disappears, they create a new one. When the world throws chaos at them, they find a way forward.

This isn't just optimism or positive thinking. It's a specific psychological trait that researchers call "Internal Locus of Control" - and it's the single most powerful predictor of career success in uncertain times.

And here's the beautiful part: It's not something you're born with.

It's something you can develop.

That's what Chapter 10 is all about. Because all the tactics in this book - from building your ikigai to mastering AI to becoming an amazing teammate - only work if you genuinely believe you have the power to use them.

So if you're ready to develop the ultimate meta-skill, the one that makes everything else possible, the one that will carry you through whatever the future throws at you...

Turn the page.

10

THE MOST IMPORTANT
LESSON OF ALL

was ten years old the first time I realized I had power.

It was a Sunday morning in January. Buffalo, New York. The kind of morning that makes you question every life choice that led you to this moment.

I'd woken up at 5 AM to deliver papers for the *Buffalo News*. The Sunday edition weighed about ten pounds each back then – stuffed with ads for grocery stores and car dealerships that nobody would read.

It was pitch black. Below freezing. Snow everywhere.

And I was a fifth-grader with frozen hands, trudging through the dark, delivering papers to houses where everyone else was still asleep.

This was my job. The same routine, day after day. Wake up. Deliver papers. Go home. Repeat.

I had no power. No agency. No control.

Or so I thought.

That morning, after finishing my route, I counted my papers. I had ten left over.

The normal thing to do? Toss them in the recycling bin and go back to bed.

But standing there in the freezing dark, my hands numb, I had a crazy idea:

What if I took these to the corner and sold them to passing cars?

Like the newsies from those old black-and-white photos. Standing on street corners, hawking papers to anyone who'd buy.

It was ridiculous. I was a kid. In the freezing cold. With newspapers nobody wanted.

But I tried it anyway.

"Buffalo News! Get your Sunday paper!"

Car after car drove past. Most ignored me. Some looked at me like I was insane.

But then one stopped. Then another. Then another.

By the time my hands were completely frozen two hours later, I had $20 in my pocket.

Twenty dollars.

That was the exact amount I usually made for an *entire week* of delivering papers.

And standing there with frozen hands and a pocket full of cash, I learned the most important lesson of my entire life:

Even when you feel like the most powerless person in the world, you always have *more* power than you realize.

THE LESSON THAT CHANGED EVERYTHING

I've been chasing that feeling ever since.

When I couldn't break into tech after seven years of trying, I didn't give up. I kept experimenting until I found a way in.

When I got sick and couldn't work for three months, I didn't accept defeat. I rebuilt my career around what actually mattered.

When I started my own business with just a $2.99 Kindle book, I didn't wait for permission. I just started.

But the moment that really proved this lesson? It wasn't when things were going well.

It was during COVID.

When Everything Falls Apart

March 2020. The world shut down overnight.

Khan Academy suddenly faced the ultimate external event: Schools were closed. Teachers were scrambling. Parents were pulling their hair out trying to homeschool. And we had no plan, no field manual for what to do next.

Meanwhile, I was stuck at home with my kids, trying to keep them entertained while doing my job from a makeshift desk in my bedroom.

Everything felt completely out of control.

And yet.

In the midst of this terrible moment, teachers and parents needed Khan Academy more than ever. Parents were losing their minds. Teachers were using their shower doors as whiteboards on Zoom calls.

We could have thrown up our hands and said: "Well, this is out of our control. Nothing we can do."

Instead, we took action.

We built out a whole series of responses: We created homeschool guides for parents in five different languages. We hosted workshops to help educators master Zoom. And we created spaces for teachers to just... breathe. (I'll never forget hosting a session where 100+ teachers joined a Zoom call just to scream together. Pure catharsis.)

The result?

Our usage went up 5X. We did some of the best work of our careers - right in the middle of the worst crisis of our generation.

Not because we could control COVID. But because we could control our *response* to it.

WHAT THIS BOOK HAS REALLY BEEN ABOUT

Here's what I haven't told you yet:

Every chapter you've read. Every framework you've learned. Every exercise you've completed.

They've all been building towards *the same thing*.

Not just job search skills. Not just AI expertise. Not just net-working tactics.

They've been building your **Internal Locus of Control** – the unshakeable belief that you control your own destiny.

Chapter 3: Start with Strengths

- You didn't wait for a career counselor to tell you what you're good at
- You took control by systematically identifying your ikigai
- You proved you can understand yourself better than any assessment

Chapter 4: Unite with Uniquely Human Skills

- You didn't just read about empathy and storytelling
- You built an actual project that required real human connection
- You proved you can create value through relationships, not just technical skills

Chapter 5: Reinforce with Relevant AI

- You didn't let AI do your thinking for you
- You learned to use it as an amplifier, not a replacement
- You proved you can master new tools without losing yourself

Chapter 6: Finish with Fellowship

- You didn't wait for networking events to find you
- You systematically built relationships with people who matter
- You proved you can create opportunities through strategic giving

Chapter 7: How to Get Your Next Job

- You didn't just spam applications and hope for the best
- You learned to win over every audience in the hiring process
- You proved you can create opportunities instead of waiting for them

Chapter 8: How to Succeed in Your Next Job

- You didn't just show up and follow orders
- You learned to become the teammate everyone wants to work with
- You proved you can shape your work environment, not just adapt to it

Chapter 9: How to Build Your Next Job

- You didn't accept that employment is your only option
- You learned to create value independently
- You proved you can build something from nothing

See the pattern?

Every single chapter. Every single story. All about the same thing.

Not waiting for permission. Not hoping things work out. Not depending on someone else to make decisions about your future.

Taking action. Making choices. Creating your own path.

That's Internal Locus of Control.

And it's the single most powerful predictor of career success - especially in uncertain times.

THE RESEARCH IS CLEAR

Study after study confirms what that frozen ten-year-old in Buffalo discovered:

People with a strong Internal Locus of Control - those who believe they control their own outcomes - consistently outperform people who believe external factors determine their fate.

They earn higher salaries. They get promoted faster. They're more satisfied with their careers. They handle setbacks better. They adapt to change more successfully.[117]

But here's what matters most: **Internal Locus of Control isn't something you're born with.**

It's something you develop through repeated experiences of taking action and seeing results.

Every time you:

- Choose a direction instead of waiting to be told
- Take a risk instead of playing it safe
- Learn from failure instead of giving up
- Create something instead of consuming
- Help someone instead of just networking

---

117 Ng, Thomas W. H., Kelly L. Sorensen, and Lillian T. Eby. "Locus of Control at Work: A Meta-Analysis." Journal of Organizational Behavior 27, no. 8 (2006): 1057-1087. https://doi.org/10.1002/job.416.

You're building your Internal Locus of Control.

You're proving to yourself: *I have power. I can make things happen. I control my destiny.*

WHY THIS MATTERS MORE THAN EVER

We're living through the biggest technological disruption since the Industrial Revolution.

AI is changing everything about how work gets done. Jobs that existed for decades are disappearing. New opportunities are emerging that didn't exist last year.

The future is genuinely uncertain.

Remember back in Chapter 2, when I told you about the wave? How there are three kinds of people when disruption hits?

- **The Deniers** - who keep building their sand castles, pretending nothing's changing
- **The Runners** - who see the wave coming and hide under the blankets
- **The Surfers** - who grab their boards and paddle out

Well, here we are. The wave isn't on the horizon anymore.
It's here.

And every single person reading this book is making a choice right now about which kind of person they're going to be.

The Deniers are still waiting for things to go back to "normal." They're hoping AI is overhyped. They're crossing their fingers that their employer will protect them.

The Runners see what's coming and they're paralyzed. They believe AI will replace them. They think they have no power. They're waiting for someone else to tell them what to do.

But the Surfers? They're already on their boards.

They see AI as a tool, not a threat. They recognize disruption as opportunity. They take action without waiting for permission.

They believe their fate is in their own hands.

Which one are you going to be?

YOUR NEXT MOVE

So here's my final challenge to you:

Don't just close this book and go back to waiting for the perfect moment.

Do something this week that proves you're ready for the wave.

Not something huge. Just something that requires you to take action without being told.

Maybe you:

- Interview someone doing your dream job and totally geek out about their journey
- Send a cold message to a Hiring Manager with a specific solution to their biggest headache
- Help a teammate with something totally outside your job description
- Set up a Calendly coaching link and start putting a value on your expertise

It doesn't matter what you choose.

What matters is that you choose.

Because every time you choose action over waiting, you're not just building skills.

You're proving something deeper.

You're proving that you're the kind of person who makes things happen. Who creates opportunities. Who takes control of their own destiny.

You're proving you're unbreakable.

GRAB YOUR BOARD

AI isn't going away. Disruption isn't going to stop. The future will keep being uncertain.

And you know what?

That's exactly when surfers thrive.

Here's what most people get wrong about surfing:

They think the surfers who catch the best waves are just lucky. Right place, right time.

But ask any real surfer and they'll tell you: **You make your own waves.**

You study the ocean. You position yourself. You read the patterns. You paddle hard when you see opportunity coming.

And when that wave arrives? You're already moving.

That's what you've been learning to do throughout this entire book.

While everyone else is standing on the beach, paralyzed by the size of the waves, you're out there - reading the patterns, positioning yourself, paddling hard.

Making your own luck.

That ten-year-old kid standing on a frozen Buffalo street corner didn't know about Internal Locus of Control or career frameworks or any of this.

He just knew one thing:

He had more power than anyone told him he had.

And so do you.

The wave is here.

Your board is ready.

Now go ride it.

GET MY SURFBOT FOR FREE!

Want to turbocharge your career - from finding the perfect AI-proof role to building your own role from scratch?

Introducing SurfBot 4000.

It's an AI bot trained on everything in this book and it's like having me as your personal coach - available 24/7 to:

- Help you apply the SURF framework to your specific situation
- Review your resume, LinkedIn profile, and cover letter
- Get you ready for massive interview success
- Troubleshoot your job search
- Plan your portfolio career

Here's how to access it:

1. Get instructions at THEJOBINSIDERS.COM/SURF
2. Review the book online to help others discover it
3. Submit the review and get instant, lifetime access to SurfBot!

Get the best of Unbreakable, on-demand!

ACKNOWLEDGMENTS

Writing a book about surviving disruption - all while *living* through one - has been quite a journey. I never would have made it without:

Rachel - for supporting every crazy career pivot, side project, and 5 AM career workshop. You believed in me before I did.

Ruby and Hannah - for reminding me what really matters when I got too caught up in the work. You're *my* North Star.

My parents - for letting me take that first newspaper job at age 10 and kicking off a life inspired by possibility, not just limitations.

Rose - for embodying everything this book teaches about taking ownership. You made The Job Insiders what it is today.

My university partners across the world - for the opportunity to come on this crazy AI journey with you and your students. Your wisdom and feedback shaped every chapter.

The people who've kicked my butt for 40+ years - from my kindergarteners in Brooklyn to my colleagues at LinkedIn and Khan Academy… and yes, even Jeff Weiner. You taught me that true success isn't about looking great when things are going well - it's about taking agency when everything's uncertain.

And you, reading this right now – for choosing to surf the wave instead of running from it. The world needs more people like you.

Thank you all for making this possible.

ABOUT THE AUTHOR

 Jeremy Schifeling has devoted his career to helping others succeed in theirs.

From teaching kindergarten in Brooklyn to recruiting top students at Teach For America to leading education marketing at LinkedIn, he's touched the lives of millions of people at every stage of their journeys.

Along the way, he's published the #1 best-selling LinkedIn and ChatGPT for Job-Seeking books, served as a career coach for military veterans at Shift.org and MBA students at the University of Michigan, and produced the most-viewed video in LinkedIn's history.

Today, Jeremy partners with 350+ universities from the Australian Graduate School of Management to the Zicklin School of Business via his AI and LinkedIn training firm, The Job Insiders.

When he's not writing about the future of work, Jeremy lives in the San Francisco Bay Area with his wife and daughters - who remind him daily that the best career advice is useless if you forget for whom and why you're working!

CONNECT WITH JEREMY

Web: thejobinsiders.com
LinkedIn: linkedin.com/in/schifeling
Email: jeremy@thejobinsiders.com

KEEP GOING.
THE WAVE ISN'T
GOING TO SURF ITSELF.